THE
RULES OF GOLF

An official
publication of the
United States
Golf Association

THE RULES OF GOLF

By

TOM WATSON

With Frank Hannigan

TimesBOOKS

The 1988 *Official Rules of Golf* was previously published by the United States
Golf Association. Copyright © 1988 by United States Golf Association.

Library of Congress Cataloging-in-Publication Data

Watson, Tom, 1949–
   The rules of golf.

   Rev. ed. of: The new rules of golf. 1st ed. c1984.
   Includes index.
   1. Golf—Rules.   I. Hannigan, Frank.   II. Watson, Tom, 1949–
New rules of golf.   III. United States Golf Association.   IV. Title.
GV971.W367   1988   796.352'02'022   87-28351
ISBN 0-8129-1729-4
ISBN 0-8129-1728-6 (pbk.)

9   8   7   6   5   4   3

Revised Edition

CONTENTS

Playing the Ball

The Putting Green

Ball Moved, Deflected or Stopped

Relief Situations and Procedure

Other Forms of Play

Administration

INTRODUCTION

The Rules of Golf are the joint responsibility of two organizations—the Royal and Ancient Golf Club of St. Andrews, Scotland (R&A) and the United States Golf Association (USGA). They jointly write and interpret the Rules, and every national golf organization, professional and amateur, defers to their judgment. An agreement exists to the effect that neither the USGA nor the R&A will act unilaterally and that amendments will be adopted only every fourth year. This book is published as the 1988 changes take effect.

This edition, like its predecessors, is not aimed at any one segment of golfers. It assumes a basic understanding of golf terminology, but beginners as well as experienced players can profit from the experience.

My point of view remains unashamedly traditional. There exists only one set of Rules and here they are. "Winter Rules," which permit the golfer to improve the lie by moving the ball, should be shunned except when it is otherwise impossible to play.

The great satisfaction of golf comes from accepting, meeting and overcoming the challenge of a singularly difficult game. Relaxing the Rules in order to make the game easier would diminish the joy that follows a great round.

That isn't to say that I think the Rules are perfect. They are man-made, and they deal with a very complicated game played on a vast and irregular playing field, so perfection isn't possible. What is perfect, though, is that the playing Rules are the same for everyone in the more than sixty nations where golf is played. That doesn't happen in other games.

Throughout this book are references to Decisions—formal and published clarifications of the Rules. Readers who want to immerse themsleves in the clarifications should obtain *Decisions on the Rules of Golf,* published annually by the USGA (Far Hills, NJ 07931—$15).

This is the third version of this book. The first two, published in 1980 and 1984, sold 230,000 copies—an astonishing total for a golf book without instruction.

My thanks again are extended to C. A. (Tony) Wimpfheimer of Random House, who proposed that there be such a book.

Over the years the manuscript has been inspected and approved by many in the USGA family. They include Bill Williams, Grant Spaeth, P. J. Boatwright, Tom Meeks, C. McDonald England and Dr. Richard Silver.

ETIQUETTE

Safety

Prior to playing a stroke or making a practice swing, the player should ensure that no one is standing close by or in a position to be hit by the club, the ball or any stones, pebbles, twigs or the like which may be moved by the stroke or swing.

Courtesy on the Course

Consideration for Other Players

The player who has the honor should be allowed to play before his opponent or fellow-competitor tees his ball.

No one should move, talk or stand close to or directly behind the ball or the hole when a player is addressing the ball or making a stroke.

In the interest of all, players should play without delay.

No player should play until the players in front are out of range.

Players searching for a ball should signal the players behind them to pass as soon as it becomes apparent that the ball will not easily be found. They should not search for five minutes before doing so. They should not continue play until the players following them have passed and are out of range.

When the play of a hole has been completed, players should immediately leave the putting green.

Priority on the Course

In the absence of special rules, two-ball matches should have precedence over and be entitled to pass any three- or four-ball match.

A single player has no standing and should give way to a match of any kind.

Any match playing a whole round is entitled to pass a match playing a shorter round.

If a match fails to keep its place on the course and loses more than one clear hole on the players in front, it should allow the match following to pass.

Care of the Course

Holes in Bunkers

Before leaving a bunker, a player should carefully fill up and smooth over all holes and footprints made by him.

Replace Divots; Repair Ball Marks and Damage by Spikes

Through the green, a player should ensure that any turf cut or displaced by him is replaced at once and pressed down and that any damage to the putting green made by a ball is carefully repaired. Damage to the putting green caused by golf shoe spikes should be repaired *on completion of the hole.*

Damage to Greens—Flagsticks, Bags, etc.

Players should ensure that, when putting down bags or the flagstick, no damage is done to the putting green and that neither they nor their caddies damage the hole by standing close to it, in handling the flagstick or in removing the ball from the hole. The flagstick should be properly replaced in the hole before the players leave the putting green. Players should not damage the putting green by leaning on their putters, particularly when removing the ball from the hole.

Golf Carts
Local notices regulating the movement of golf carts should be strictly observed.

Damage Through Practice Swings
In taking practice swings, players should avoid causing damage to the course, particularly the tees, by removing divots.

The section on Etiquette reveals the rules of conduct which guide golfers in their relationships with one another and with the course. Ours is a sensitive, perhaps even a fragile, game. For golf to prosper or be fun to play (which may be the highest form of prosperity), golfers have to behave decently. The game could not survive public displays of temper or acts of recrimination against a tee or putting green.

The relationship between the golfer and the course is fascinating. I can't think of another sport in which the playing arena must be maintained, in part, by the players. In golf we take it for granted that the player has the responsibililty for performing the elementary housekeeping chores of replacing divots, repairing ball marks and smoothing bunkers.

There is, howerver, a provision of the Etiquette section which is often ignored, or so it seems to me. That's the one that reads: "In the interest of all, players should play without delay."

Slow play is golf's disease. Four players in the same group should not need more than four hours to play 18 holes of golf. The five-hour round is a horror, and it says much for the appeal of the game that, facing the prospect of a wait on every tee, golfers go right on playing.

I don't think there's any correlation between score and pace of play. It's not necessary to agonize over shots in order to shoot sub-par scores. At the same time, the high-handicap player has no excuse for dawdling. I have friends who can't break 100, but we can play together without feeling that we're holding one another up.

I see most of the time wasted on the putting greens, both on the PGA Tour and in everyday golf. A golfer should prepare to putt as soon as he reaches a green, not when it's his turn. The time between the putts of two players should seldom be more than fifteen or twenty seconds.

I have a reputation for being one of the fastest players on the pro tour. I began to play golf with my father when I was eight years old and with the clear-cut understanding that I was more than welcome provided I kept up. So I became a fast player at a very early age.

3

DEFINITIONS

DEFINITIONS

It's impossible to understand the Rules without knowing the Definitions. The Definitions are basic. They exist because many key words and special terms in the Rules are not those we use in everyday language and must therefore be clarified.

Golfers tend to resort to the Rules only when they have a problem and are in a hurry for an answer. They'll run into a phrase such as "through the green" and the mind tends to boggle. It doesn't help, of course, that "through the green" is often misused by television commentators to apply to balls hit *beyond* the green, when it means something entirely different.

Or take the very word "stroke." Many a friendship has been strained over a discussion as to whether or not a stroke has actually been made. It's essential to the peaceful resolution of such a discussion to realize that a stroke applies only to the *forward* movement of a club.

The Definitions follow, punctuated by occasional comments which are inserted for the purpose of, if you'll pardon the expression, defining the Definitions.

Addressing the Ball

A player has "addressed the ball" when he has taken his *stance* and has also grounded his club, except that in a *hazard,* a player has addressed the ball when he has taken his stance.

Advice

"Advice" is any counsel or suggestion which could influence a player in determining his play, the choice of a club or the method of making a *stroke.*

Information on the Rules or on matters of public information, such as the position of hazards or the flagstick on the putting green, is not advice.

The second paragraph says you're not asking for "advice" when you say "Where's the hole?" When the answer comes back "It's in the back of the green," that's not giving "advice" either. But beware. There are some tricky Decisions on "advice" summarized under Rule 8.

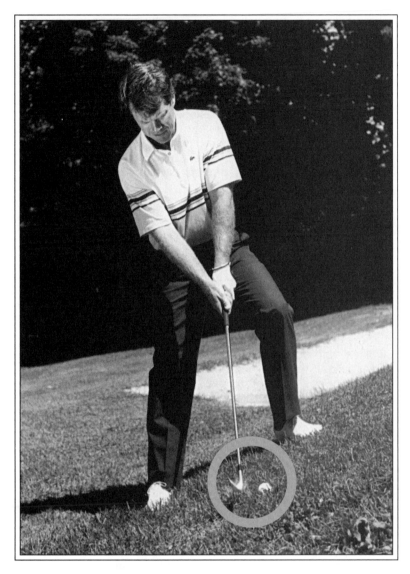

Don't Always Address a Ball

If a ball is on a slope, or perched on high grass, anywhere outside a hazard, it makes sense to play the next stroke without addressing the ball, because if the ball moves after address, the player is deemed to have caused it to move and incurs a penalty stroke. Note that I have not addressed the ball because the club has not been grounded. If the ball moves and I haven't caused it to move, there is no penalty and I would play the ball from where it then lies. This advice doesn't apply within a hazard, where the act of address is completed as soon as the stance is taken. (R. 18)

See "Move or Moved."

See "Holed."

See "Lost Ball."

A ball is "in play" as soon as the player has made a *stroke* on the *teeing ground.* It remains in play until holed out, except when it is *lost out of bounds,* or lifted, or another ball has been substituted under an applicable Rule; a ball so substituted becomes the ball in play.

Ball Deemed to Move

Ball Holed

Ball Lost

Ball in Play

There can only be one ball "in play" for one player at one time. If a player's ball heads in the direction of a water hazard and the player drops and plays another ball, the second ball is then "in play." If the player then finds the original ball to be playable and plays it, he has played a "wrong ball."

Bunker

A "bunker" is a *hazard* consisting of a prepared area of ground, often a hollow, from which turf or soil has been removed and replaced with sand or the like. Grass-covered ground bordering or within the bunker is not part of the bunker. The margin of a bunker extends vertically downwards, but not upwards.

If you insist on calling it a "sand trap," you've fallen into the trap of substituting common usage for common sense. The phrase "sand trap" does not occur in the Rules. It's a "bunker."

Caddie

A "caddie" is one who carries or handles a player's clubs during play and otherwise assists him in accordance with the Rules.

When one caddie is employed by more than one player, he is always deemed to be the caddie of the player whose ball is involved, and *equipment* carried by him is deemed to be that player's equipment, except when the caddie acts upon specific directions of another player, in which case he is considered to be that other player's caddie.

Since caddies often carry two bags, and they are often the bags of opponents, it's necessary to sort out who is penalized when a caddie breaks the Rules. If a caddie, indicating the line of putt for one of his players, touches that line with a flagstick, the player who was about to putt is penalized.

Casual Water

"Casual water" is any temporary accumulation of water on the *course* which is visible before or after the player takes his *stance* and is not in a *water hazard.* Snow and ice are either casual water or *loose impediments,* at the option of the player except that manufactured ice is an *obstruction.* Dew is not casual water.

The specification that manufactured ice is an obstruction is a 1988 fine-tuning change illustrating how the Rules evolve from odd incidents. Ben Crenshaw found his ball in a cluster of ice cubes during the 1977 U.S. Open. He and the USGA official on the spot were perplexed because the relief procedures from casual water and movable obstructions (man-made objects) are different.

Committee

The "Committee" is the committee in charge of the competition or, if the matter does not arise in a competition, the committee in charge of the *course.*

In everyday play the Committee is not likely to be available. The golf professional is usually authorized to act on behalf of the Committee.

Competitor

A "competitor" is a player in a stroke competition. A "fellow-competitor" is any person with whom the competitor plays. Neither is *partner* of the other.

In stroke play foursome and four-ball competitions, where the context so admits, the word "competitor" or "fellow-competitor" shall be held to include his partner.

"Competitor" is a nice old-fashioned and useful word which, like "bunker," doesn't get the respect it deserves. The people with whom you are playing in stroke play are "fellow-competitors." Calling them "playing partners" is inaccurate and can lead to misunderstandings, since the word "partner" suggests someone with whom you are in business and whom you can assist.

Course

The "course" is the whole area within which play is permitted. See Rule 33-2.

Equipment

"Equipment" is anything used, worn or carried by or for the player except any ball he has played and any small object, such as a coin or a tee, when used to mark the position of a ball or the extent of an area in which a ball is to be dropped. Equipment includes a golf cart, whether or not motorized. If such a cart is shared by more than one player, its status under the Rules is the same as that of a caddie employed by more than one player. See "Caddie."

Golf carts are tough on the Rules, just as they are on the turf of our courses. The problems that stem from a cart deflecting or moving a ball are myriad. They are, however, resolved in two Decisions. Here they are:

Ball Moved by Golf Cart Shared by Two Players

"Under the Definition of 'Equipment,' equipment includes a golf cart, whether or not motorized. If two players share a golf cart, the cart and everything in it are, for purposes of applying the Rules, deemed to be the equipment of the player whose ball is involved, except that, when the cart is being driven or pulled by one of the players, the cart and everything in it is considered to be that player's equipment.

"Thus, for example, in a singles match, if A and B are sharing a cart and the cart moves A's ball which was at rest, A would be penalized one stroke if he was driving or pulling the cart (Rule 18-2a). B would be penalized one stroke if he was driving or pulling the cart (Rule 18-3b), unless the incident occurred during search (Rule 18-3a)."

Ball Deflected or Stopped by Golf Cart Shared by Two Players

". . . In a singles match, if A and B are sharing a cart and A's ball in motion is deflected or stopped by the cart, A loses the hole (Rule

9

19-2a) unless the cart is being driven or pulled by B when the incident occurs. If B is driving or pulling the cart, there is no penalty, and A would have the option of playing his ball as it lies or replaying the stroke (Rule 19-3b).

"In terms of this Decision, a golf cart is not 'being driven or pulled' when it is stationary or unoccupied; in such circumstances, therefore, it is deemed to be the equipment of the player whose ball is involved."

Fellow-Competitor | See "Competitor."

Flagstick | The "flagstick" is a movable straight indicator, with or without bunting or other material attached, centered in the hole to show its position. It shall be circular in cross-section.

Forecaddie | A "forecaddie" is one who is employed by the Committee to indicate to players the position of balls during play. He is an *outside agency.*

Ground Under Repair | "Ground under repair" is any portion of the *course* so marked by order of the Committee or so declared by its authorized representative. It includes material piled for removal and a hole made by a greenkeeper, even if not so marked. Stakes and lines defining ground under repair are in such ground. The margin of ground under repair extends vertically downwards, but not upwards.

Note 1: *Grass cuttings and other material left on the course which have been abandoned and are not intended to be removed are not ground under repair unless so marked.*

Note 2. *The Committee may make a Local Rule prohibiting play from ground under repair.*

When Is a Ball in Ground Under Repair?
This ball is in an area marked ground under repair because it touches the line. I'd be entitled to take relief even if the ball was outside the area, because my stance caused me to stand on the line or within the marked ground.
(R. 25)

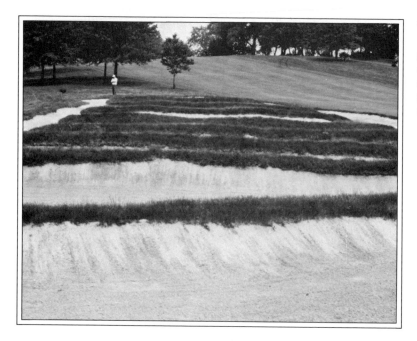

Grass in a Bunker
The Rules allow you to ground your club in a bunker in a grassy area within the bunker. Grass-covered ground within a bunker is not considered part of the hazard.

Ground under repair is customarily and best defined by white lines. When a ball touches the white line it is considered in ground under repair and the relief offered in Rule 25 can be obtained.

Why would a Committee want to make a Local Rule prohibiting play from ground under repair, as contemplated in Note 2? Because some areas—recently seeded or sodded—need protection.

Here's an interpretation clarifying ground under repair:

● Is a rut or a groove made by a maintenance vehicle considered a hole made by a greenkeeper?

Answer: No, but a player whose ball is in a deep rut would be justified in asking the Committee to declare the rut to be ground under repair, and the Committee would be justified in doing so.

Since a representative of the Committee is seldom on the spot, there are other ways available of handling such a problem. If it's stroke play, consider a second ball under Rule 3-3. In match play, if the opponent agrees that the rut should be ground under repair, treat it that way.

A "hazard" is any _bunker_ or _water hazard._	**Hazards**
The "hole" shall be 4¼ inches (108 mm) in diameter and at least 4 inches (100 mm) deep. If a lining is used, it shall be sunk at least 1 inch (25 mm) below the _putting green_ surface unless the nature of the soil makes it impraticable to do so; its outer diameter shall not exceed 4¼ inches (108 mm).	**Hole**
A ball is "holed" when it is at rest within the circumference of the hole and all of it is below the level of the lip of the hole.	**Holed**

Honor

The side entitled to play first from the *teeing ground* is said to have the "honor."

Lateral Water Hazard

A "lateral water hazard" is a *water hazard* or that part of a water hazard so situated that it is not possible or is deemed by the Committee to be impracticable to drop a ball behind the water hazard in accordance with Rule 26-1b.

That part of a water hazard to be played as a lateral water hazard should be distinctively marked.

Note: *Lateral water hazards should be defined by red stakes or lines.*

The problem with understanding this definition is that a "lateral water hazard" does not necessarily have to run lateral, or parallel, to the line of play. It's up to the Committee to make the distinction, and the Committee should be guided by the principle of whether or not it's fair or practicable to drop behind the hazard and keep the spot at which the ball last crossed the margin between the player and the hole. If not, the hazard should be categorized a "lateral" so that the player can avail himself of the extra options expressed in Rule 26-1c.

Loose Impediments

"Loose impediments" are natural objects such as stones, leaves, twigs, branches and the like, dung, worms and insects and casts or heaps made by them, provided they are not fixed or growing, are not solidly embedded and do not adhere to the ball.

Sand and loose soil are loose impediments on the *putting green,* but not elsewhere.

Snow and ice are either *casual water* or loose impediments, at the option of the player except that manufactured ice is an *obstruction.*

Dew is not a loose impediment.

A query lodged with the USGA led to one of the classic Decisions. Is a half-eaten pear in front of a ball in a bunker considered a natural object or an artificial object? If it's natural (and therefore a loose impediment), it can't be moved; if it's artificial (and thus an "obstruction"), it can be removed without penalty under Rule 24. The bunker in which the pear was lodged was not in close proximity to a pear tree.

Answer: If the player removed the pear, she violated Rule 13-4, the penalty for which is: Match play—Loss of hole; Stroke play—Two strokes.

A pear is a natural object (an obstruction must be artificial). When detached from a tree it is a loose impediment. The facts that a pear has been half-eaten and there is no pear tree in the vicinity do not alter the status of the pear.

Loose impediments may be transformed into obstructions through processes of construction or manufacturing. For example, a log (loose impediment) that has been split and has had legs attached to it has been changed by construction into a bench (obstruction).

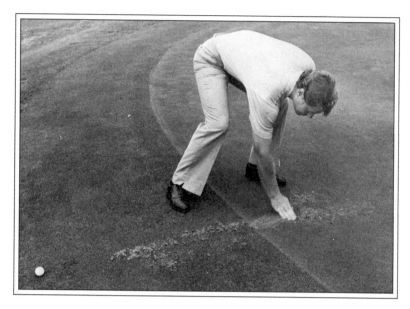

Sand Can't Always Be Removed

Sand has been splashed from a bunker onto both the putting green and the apron just off the green. Both areas are on my line to the hole and might affect the roll. Nevertheless, the sand off the green is not a loose impediment and may not be moved; the sand on the green is a loose impediment and may be removed. (R. 23)

A ball is "lost" if

a. It is not found or identified as his by the player within five minutes after the player's side or his or their caddies have begun to search for it; or

b. The player has put another ball into play under the Rules, even though he may not have searched for the original ball; or

c. The player has played any stroke with a *provisional ball* from the place where the original ball is likely to be or from a point nearer the hole than that place, whereupon the provisional ball becomes the *ball in play.*

Time spent in playing a *wrong ball* is not counted in the five-minute period allowed for search.

Lost Ball

Here's what some key Decisions on the subject of lost balls say:

• A player searches for his ball for two minutes after hitting a wild fairway wood shot, declares his ball is lost and heads back toward the original spot. Before he drops another ball and within the five-minute search period, his caddie finds his first ball.

Answer: As the player had not put another ball in play under the Rules, he could play the first ball.

• What happens in stroke play when a player searches for a ball for less than five minutes, gives up the search, returns to the tee and plays another ball? Then the original ball is found, the player picks up the second ball and he plays the first.

Answer: The original was lost when the player put the second ball in play—no matter how long the search. When he lifted the second ball he violated Rule 18-2 (one-stroke penalty). When he played a stroke with the original ball he played a wrong ball (two strokes under Rule 15-3). Finally, if he doesn't rectify the mistake by replacing and playing the second ball before he plays from the next tee, he's disqualified.

• Jimmy Thomson, reputedly the longest hitter in the world during the 1930s, asked how to rule when two players are playing identical balls, *i.e.*, balls of the same brand and marking and with the same numbers. The balls come to rest very close together, and the players are not sure of the ownership of either.

Answer: It may seem harsh, but both balls are to be treated as lost, since neither player can identify one as his. A pencil mark or a dot made by a marking pen in a dimple is all it takes to identify a ball properly.

• On a par-3 hole, in a stroke-play event, a player hit wildly and, thinking his original might be lost, played a provisional ball. The result with the provisional ball was excellent. In fact, it came to rest one inch from the hole. Must the player search for the original ball?

Answer: No. He can tap the ball near the hole in for a 4.

• An incident on the tour involving Miller Barber led to these two:

A player is reasonably certain that his ball is high up in a tree but he can't see it and therefore can't identify it. Answer: The ball is lost.

• A player can see a ball in a tree but can't retrieve it to identify it as his. Answer: The ball is lost, which means the player is not allowed to treat it as unplayable; he must suffer the stroke-and-distance penalty. That actually happened to me on the 18th hole at Cypress Point in the 1983 Crosby Tournament. I could see a ball, which was probably mine, high up in a tree, but since I couldn't identify it as mine I had to go back to the tee instead of declaring it unplayable and dropping it near the base of the tree.

You may recall seeing that happen to Tommy Nakajima at the 1987 U.S. Open. His ball seemed surely to have been swallowed by a huge tree near the 18th green at the Olympic Club, but he had to take the stroke-and-distance penalty because he could not find and identify it.

Marker

A "marker" is one who is appointed by the Committee to record a *competitor's* score in stroke play. He may be a *fellow-competitor*. He is not a *referee*.

The marker in stroke play today is invariably a fellow-competitor. On the PGA Tour you may have noticed someone, usually in a uniform, walking with each group of players and recording scores. Her function is to report the scores at the end of each hole to a communicator using a phone or radio. The scores she reports are the source material for television and scoreboards, but they are not official.

There's no such thing as a marker in match play. Keeping a hole-by-hole card in match play is a useful way of tracking the match, but the card has no official status.

Matches

See "Sides and Matches."

Move or Moved

A ball is deemed to have "moved" if it leaves its position and comes to rest in any other place.

A ball has not moved if it only jiggles or oscillates.

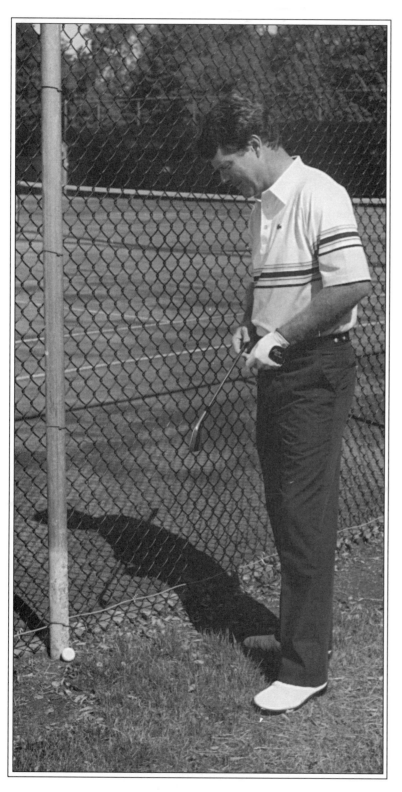

No Relief from Boundary Fence or Stakes

Even though they are artificial objects, out-of-bounds fences and their posts are not obstructions. Moreover, boundary fences, posts and stakes are regarded as "things fixed" and may not be moved. In this situation, I can attempt a difficult stroke or declare the ball unplayable. (R. 28)

15

Observer | An "observer" is one who is appointed by the Committee to assist a *referee* to decide questions of fact and to report to him any breach of a Rule. An observer should not attend the flagstick, stand at or mark the position of the hole, or lift the ball or mark its position.

Obstruction | An "obstruction" is anything artificial, including the artificial surfaces and sides of roads and paths and manufactured ice, except:

a. Objects defining *out of bounds,* such as walls, fences, stakes and railings;

b. Any part of an immovable artificial object which is out of bounds; and

c. Any construction declared by the Committee to be an integral part of the course.

The Committee has the latitude to preserve the character of a hole which might be lost if free relief was given from something artificial on that hole. The artificial construction is then classified as "an integral part of the course." The best-known case occurs on the 17th hole —the Road Hole—of the Old Course at St. Andrews in Scotland. When you miss the green to the right, the ball invariably winds up on the blacktop road adjacent to and well below the green. When I'm on the road, I pray to get down in three. The road makes the 17th hole at St. Andrews one of the great par-4 holes anywhere.

Out of Bounds | "Out of bounds" is ground on which play is prohibited.

When out of bounds is defined by reference to stakes or a fence or as being beyond stakes or a fence, the out of bounds line is determined by the nearest inside points of the stakes or fence posts at ground level excluding angled supports.

When out of bounds is defined by a line on the ground, the line itself is out of bounds.

The out of bounds line extends vertically upwards and downwards.

A ball is out of bounds when all of it lies out of bounds.

A player may stand out of bounds to play a ball lying within bounds.

Outside Agency | An "outside agency" is any agency not part of the match, or, in stroke play, not part of a competitor's side, and includes a referee, a marker, an observer or a forecaddie. Neither wind nor water is an outside agency.

Golf balls are occasionally deflected or moved by alien objects and beings such a dogs, spectators and trash containers. Those are called "outside agencies," and within the body of the Rules you'll find what to do, depending on the circumstances, when an outside agency intrudes.

Partner | A "partner" is a player associated with another player on the same side.

In Bounds and Out of Bounds

The out-of-bounds line is determined by the inside points of fence posts at ground level. A ball is out of bounds only when all of it lies out of bounds. Rules of Golf officials sometimes decide close calls by stretching a string from post to post. The ball at the bottom is in bounds; the ball at left is out of bounds. (R. 27)

17

In a threesome, foursome, best-ball or four-ball match where the context so admits, the word "player" shall be held to include his partner.

Penalty Stroke

A "penalty stroke" is one added to the score of a player or *side* under certain Rules. In a threesome or foursome, penalty strokes do not affect the order of play.

Provisional Ball

A "provisional ball" is a ball played under Rule 27-2 for a ball which may be *lost* outside a *water hazard* or may be *out of bounds.*

The phrase "provisional ball" is often confused with "second ball" in Rule 3-3. The former is a ball you may play in order to save time when your ball may be lost (not in a water hazard) or out of bounds, but you're not sure; the latter is a ball you are allowed to play in stroke play when you are doubtful of your rights or the proper procedure.

Key point: You may not play a provisional ball for the reason that the ball may be in a water hazard.

Putting Green

The "putting green" is all ground of the hole being played which is specially prepared for putting or otherwise defined as such by the Committee. A ball is on the putting green when any part of it touches the putting green.

An "apron" or "collar" (words that do not appear in the Rules) is a narrow strip cut nearly as low as the green but not considered part of the putting green.

Referee

A "referee" is one who is appointed by the Committee to accompany players to decide questions of fact and apply the Rules of Golf. He shall act on any breach of a Rule which he observes or is reported to him.

A referee should not attend the flagstick, stand at or mark the position of the hole, or lift the ball or mark its position.

Very few golfers ever have the opportunity to play with a referee accompanying them. It's too bad, because the presence of a referee seems to put the game on a slightly higher plane. Referees can enhance the final matches of club championships, provided they're competent. The USGA offers a fascinating booklet for the bargain price of $1 on the subject called "Duties of Officials Under the Rules of Golf." (Write to the USGA, Far Hills, NJ 07931.)

Rub of the Green

A "rub of the green" occurs when a ball in motion is accidentally deflected or stopped by any *outside agency* (see Rule 19-1).

Rule

The term "Rule" includes Local Rules made by the Committee under Rule 33-8a.

18 **Sides and Matches**

SIDE: A player, or two or more players who are *partners.*

SINGLE: A match in which one plays against another.

THREESOME: A match in which one plays against two, and each side plays one ball.

FOURSOME: A match in which two play against two, and each side plays one ball.

THREE-BALL: A match in which three play against one another, each playing his own ball.

BEST-BALL: A match in which one plays against the better ball of two or the best ball of three players.

FOUR-BALL: A match in which two play their better ball against the better ball of two other players.

I'm a traditionalist and am therefore among the minority in the United States who believe we should cling to the proper usage of the terms in this Definition and fight the good, if losing, fight against the bastardization of these terms. Thus:

• A threesome is not three who are playing together; it's a form of competition that is virtually extinct. ("Twosome" is an ugly word often, and mistakenly, applied to two players paired in stroke play.)

• A foursome is a fascinating form of competition in which partners play alternating strokes. It is not four players who are playing together. This form of play is sometimes and unnecessarily referred to as a "Scotch Foursome."

• A four-ball is by far the most popular form of golf played in this country. Alas, too often it's called a "best-ball," which, again, is an interesting but out-of-vogue kind of match covered in Rule 30.

Stance

Taking the "stance" consists in a player placing his feet in position for and preparatory to making a *stroke*.

Stipulated Round

The "stipulated round" consists of playing the holes of the course in their correct sequence unless otherwise authorized by the Committee. The number of holes in a stipulated round is 18 unless a smaller number is authorized by the Committee. As to extension of stipulated round in match play, see Rule 2-3.

This gives us an excuse to paraphrase a celebrated Stipulated Round question and answer.

• In match play, two players were so busy talking that they failed to play two holes. They did not realize the omission until the results of the match were posted and they wondered why their scores were so good. It was too late in the day to send them out again to play the whole 18, and to wait until the following day to replay their match would have delayed the whole flight and upset the tournament schedule. The Committee sent them out immediately after their error was discovered to play the two holes they had left out, and was anxious to know whether or not this was correct. Unfortunately, those two holes changed the result of the match.

What is the correct ruling in such a case?

Answer: The Committee's decision is final (see Rule 34-3). However, the Committee should *not* have directed that the two omitted

The Teeing Ground

The teeing ground is a rectangular area two club-lengths in depth. You can tee your ball anywhere in that rectangle. You're not required to stand within it. I've chosen to stand outside the teeing ground in the bottom picture because I feel that setup makes it easier to stay out of the trouble that lurks on the left side of the hole.

holes be played belatedly. The result of the match should have been allowed to stand as originally posted—see Rule 2-5. Had the players agreed to play less than the stipulated round, both would have been subject to disqualification—see Rule 1-3.

Stroke
A "stroke" is the forward movement of the club made with the intention of fairly striking at and moving the ball, but if a player checks his downswing voluntarily before the clubhead reaches the ball he is deemed not to have made the stroke.

The second part of the "stroke" definition was added in 1988. It incorporates into the definition what was a long-standing Decision. It's not a stroke if the player can stop before the clubhead reaches the ball.

Here's what some Decisions say about strokes:

- A player disgustedly raps his ball off the green after missing a short putt. The player must replace the ball since the action is not considered a stroke. Penalty: one stroke.
- A player plays a stroke at his ball but then discovers it was out of bounds. Answer: He played a wrong ball since a ball out of bounds is no longer in play.
- The weaker partner in a foursomes match purposely "whiffed" her ball rather than attempt to carry a water hazard. Answer: Nice try, but that was not a stroke since it was made without intent to hit the ball. When the partner played after the "whiff" the team played out of order and lost the hole.

Teeing Ground
The "teeing ground" is the starting place for the hole to be played. It is a rectangular area two club-lengths in depth, the front and sides of which are defined by the outside limits of two tee-markers. A ball is outside the teeing ground when all of it lies outside the teeing ground.

This is the first time we run into a reference to "club-lengths," which occurs time and again within the Rules proper. The term is used instead of a specific distance, such as "six feet," because golfers aren't expected to carry tape measures. Any club is acceptable and, obviously, a driver is the best candidate, since it will make for the biggest rectangular area.

Through the Green
"Through the green" is the whole area of the *course* except: a. The *teeing ground* and *putting green* of the hole being played; and b. All *hazards* on the course.

The important phrase "through the green" recurs throughout the Rules. It's a phrase that encompasses most of the course but not the tee of the hole being played or the putting green of the hole being played or any hazard. Everything else is "through the green." The distinctions are often critical. For example, if your ball is just off the green and there's casual water between your ball and the hole, you get no relief—that is, you don't get to move it, since the ball is "through the green." But if the ball is on the putting green in the same circumstance, a special kind of relief is available under Rule 25-1.

Water Hazard

A "water hazard" is any sea, lake, pond, river, ditch, surface drainage ditch or other open water course (whether or not containing water) and anything of a similar nature.

All ground or water within the margin of a water hazard is part of the water hazard. The margin of a water hazard extends vertically upwards and downwards. Stakes and lines defining the margins of water hazards are in the hazards.

Note: Water hazards (other than lateral water hazards) should be defined by yellow stakes or lines.

Stakes used to define hazards are obstructions and may be removed when they interfere, but as the Definition of "out of bounds" reveals, stakes defining boundaries may not be moved.

There is some understandable confusion about the proper names for and distinctions between types of water hazards. Think of it this way: there are only two kinds. The most common is, quite simply, a "water hazard," and is often called a "regular water hazard." The other is a "lateral water hazard." The distinction is important because the relief procedure from lateral water hazards is more generous.

Wrong Ball

A "wrong ball" is any ball other than:

a. The *ball in play.*

b. A *provisional ball* or

c. In stroke play, a second ball played under Rule 3-3 or Rule 20-7b.

Note: Ball in play includes a ball substituted for the ball in play when the player is proceeding under an applicable Rule which does not permit substitution.

THE
RULES
OF PLAY

THE GAME

RULE 1

THE GAME

1-1
General

The Game of Golf consists in playing a ball from the <u>teeing ground</u> into the hole by a <u>stroke</u> or successive strokes in accordance with the Rules.

1-2
Exerting Influence on Ball

No player or caddie shall take any action to influence the position or the movement of a ball except in accordance with the Rules.

PENALTY FOR BREACH OF RULE 1-2:
Match play—Loss of hole; Stroke play—Two strokes.
Note: *In the case of a serious breach of Rule 1-2, the Committee may impose a penalty of disqualification.*

1-3
Agreement to Waive Rules

Players shall not agree to exclude the operation of any Rule or to waive any penalty incurred.

PENALTY FOR BREACH OF RULE 1-3:
Match play—Disqualification of both sides; Stroke play—Disqualification of competitors concerned.

(Agreeing to play out of turn in stroke play—see Rule 10-2c.)

1-4
Points Not Covered by Rules

If any point in dispute is not covered by the Rules, the decision shall be made in accordance with equity.

1-1. General

The Rules of Golf begin with a straightforward definition of the game itself. One sentence of twenty-seven words does the job.

This is the place you should begin to pick out the key words and phrases used in the Definitions and to familiarize yourself with the precise language used throughout the Rules. There are no fewer than five checkpoints in this sentence of twenty-seven words:

- "Playing *a* ball" means playing *one* ball. You may not change to a shiny new ball once you've cleared a water hazard or landed safely on a putting green.
- "The 'teeing ground,'" according to the Definition, "is the starting place for the hole to be played," and its dimensions are specific.
- "Into the hole" reveals that, in stroke play, if you fail to hole out, you have failed to play the game—and that you're disqualified.
- "By successive strokes" calls for an understanding of a stroke, which according to the Definition "is the forward movement of the club made with the intention of fairly striking at and moving the ball." Incidentally, Richard Peters came to play in the very first U.S. Amateur Championship in 1895 intending to putt with a billiard cue. There is no such thing as a stroke made with a billiard cue, because a billiard cue isn't a club.
- "In accordance with the Rules" is what this book is about. In order to understand and enjoy the game you *must* know the Rules.

1-2. Exerting Influence on Ball

Some examples illustrating what Rule 1-2 means (taking "any action to influence the position or the movement of a ball") are found in Decisions.

- A player purposely steps on and damages (or improves) his opponent's line of putt. Violation!
- A player in a professional event in Wales ingeniously placed his bag parallel to the line of short putt to shield the line from the wind. Violation!
- In the California Amateur Championship at stroke play a competitor who had holed out repaired spike marks on the line of putt of a fellow-competitor. Violation! The player who did the repair job is penalized two strokes. If the player whose line was improved sanctioned the repair job, he too should be penalized two strokes, but under Rule 13-2. If it's found that there was an agreement between the two to repair damage on each other's line of putt, both should be disqualified under Rule 1-3 for having agreed to waive a Rule.
- A player's putt hangs on the lip of the hole. He jumps as high as he can, three feet from the cup. The ball falls in. Violation!
- As an act of sportsmanship, a player removes a loose impediment —a stone or leaf—directly in front of an opponent's ball in a bunker. No matter what the motive, the player lost the hole.
- A caddie used a towel to mop up a pool of water between the player and the hole but the water was on the apron—not on a putting green. The player violated Rule 13-2 as he allowed his caddie to improve his line of play.

1-3. Agreement to Waive Rules

Rule 1-3 expresses the principle that golf is meant to be the same game for everyone with the same code of Rules and the same set of penalties. It becomes a different game, for instance, when opponents agree that they'll concede each other every putt "within the leather." They've made an agreement to ignore Rule 1-1, and both should be disqualified.

Rule 1-3 is vital to the integrity of the game, so the interpretations have been consistently and properly strict. Key decisions:

• In a match player A, who won the last hole, says to B, "You hit first. I don't want the honor." B agrees and plays first.

Answer: They've agreed to waive Rule 10-1, which provides that the last player who won a hole is to play first on every hole until he loses one, and both are to be disqualified.

• A naughty thing happened in a regional competition. During a stroke-play round, a competitor failed to hole out once but continued to play the round. Her marker (another competitor in the same pairing) observed the violation but signed the score card anyway. Both were well aware of the violation.

Answer: Failing to hole out in stroke play is a violation calling for disqualification. In this case both are disqualified on the basis that they agreed to waive rule 1-1.

• A player and his opponent agreed before a match that they'd repair spike marks on each other's lines of putt. Both should be disqualified for agreeing to waive Rule 16-1a (Touching Line of Putt) even though it was match play and no other player was directly involved.

1-4. Points Not Covered by Rules

No set of rules can cover every possible situation, and therefore it is sometimes necessary to rule "in equity." Here's a sampling:

• This actually happened. A woman took a hefty cut at a ball on an embankment. At first she couldn't find her ball, but then saw it stuck in the face of the club, held firmly by wet clay.

Answer: She should drop the ball as near as possible to the spot where the club was when the ball stuck to it. Here there is no penalty but, naturally, the stroke she made was counted.

• A player's ball came to rest so near a bird's nest that he could not play a stroke without damaging it. The decision-makers, in what some think was an out-of-character burst of humanity, say that the ball can be dropped away from the nest without penalty.

• As A was making his backswing B *accidentally* dropped a ball which rolled within six inches of A's ball. Poor A, startled, topped his shot and asked to be allowed to replay his stroke "in equity." He wasn't, because "distractions are a common occurence which players must accept."

• As a player stepped into a bunker to play a shot, she noticed a rattlesnake near her ball. What to do?

Answer: It's not reasonable to expect a player to play from such a dangerous situation. The player is allowed to place a ball without penalty in the hazard, or in a similar nearby hazard, in a situation she does not regard as dangerous, as near as possible to the spot where the ball lay and in a lie similar to that which it originally occupied. The same applies to bees and wasps; indeed, a similar ruling was made for players in a bunker infested by yellow jackets in the 1949 Amateur Championship at the Oak Hill Country Club, Rochester, N.Y.

• A caddie for Lancy Smith, one of the best American women amateurs, accidentally kicked a coin marking the position of her opponent's ball closer to the hole.

Answer: The coin should be replaced as close as possible to the spot where it lay without penalty to anyone. A ball-marker is a movable obstruction and does not have the same status as a ball in play.

RULE 2

MATCH PLAY

2-1 Winner of Hole

In match play the game is played by holes.

Except as otherwise provided in the Rules, a hole is won by the side which holes its ball in the fewer strokes. In a handicap match the lower net score wins the hole.

The reckoning of holes is kept by the terms: so many "holes up" or "all square," and so many "to play."

A side is "dormie" when it is as many holes up as there are holes remaining to be played.

2-2 Halved Hole

A hole is halved if each side holes out in the same number of strokes.

When a player has holed out and his opponent has been left with a stroke for the half, if the player thereafter incurs a penalty, the hole is halved.

2-3 Winner of Match

A match (which consists of a stipulated round, unless otherwise decreed by the Committee) is won by the side which is leading by a number of holes greater than the number of holes remaining to be played.

The Committee may, for the purpose of settling a tie, extend the stipulated round to as many holes as are required for a match to be won.

2-4 Concession of Next Stroke, Hole or Match

When the opponent's ball is at rest or is deemed to be at rest under Rule 16-2, the player may concede the opponent to have holed out with his next stroke and the ball may be removed by either side with a club or otherwise.

A player may concede a hole or a match at any time prior to the conclusion of the hole or the match.

Concession of a stroke, hole or match may not be declined or withdrawn.

2-5 Claims

In match play, if a doubt or dispute arises between the players and no duly authorized representative of the Committee is available within a reasonable time, the players shall continue the match without delay. Any claim, if it is to be considered by the Committee, must be made before any player in the match plays from the next teeing ground or, in the case of the last hole of the match, before all players in the match leave the putting green.

27

No later claim shall be considered unless it is based on facts previously unknown to the player making the claim and the player making the claim had been given wrong information (Rules 6-2a and 9) by an opponent. In any case, no later claim shall be considered after the result of the match has been officially announced, unless the Committee is satisfied that the opponent knew he was giving wrong information.

2-6
General Penalty

The penalty for a breach of a Rule in match play is loss of hole except when otherwise provided.

One of golf's special appeals is that it can be played two ways. The outcome can be determined on the basis of holes won—match play—or by total number of strokes—stroke play. Arguments about the more valid form of play go on endlessly. I prefer stroke play, but I do not quarrel with the contention that match play (which is the only way golf was played for hundreds of years) is fascinating, calls for a different strategic approach and, above all, is intensely personal.

Rule 2-1 defines match play as the form of the game in which score is kept by the winning of holes rather than by total strokes. Rule 2-2 is a logical exception to the customary penalties in match play. There are occasions when, for example, player A has holed out in 4 and his opponent is left with a putt for a 4. Player A then violates a Rule—let's say he inadvertently moves the opponent's ball. That violation calls for a one-stroke penalty, which is not assessed in this instance. Since the best his opponent could possibly do is to make the putt and tie the hole, Rule 2-2 reasonably asserts that the hole is halved.

What about the phrase "stipulated round" in Rule 2-3? Again, the Definitions are critical. The "stipulated round" requires that the holes be played in the correct sequence. A Decision tells how two players in a match somehow got lost after six holes and proceeded to play three holes other than the 7th, 8th and 9th. They then discovered the error and asked what to do.

Answer: Ignore the results of the three holes played out of sequence, go back and resume the match on the 7th hole and replay the holes played in error when they are reached.

Remember that the "stipulated round" starts on the 1st hole—not the 10th. Opponents in a club match who find that the 1st tee is backed up but the 10th is open need the approval of the Committee in order to begin a match on the back nine.

Concessions should be loud and clear. Once a putt is conceded, that's it. The player is considered to have holed out on his next stroke. The concession may not be recalled or declined. (If the player nonetheless putts and misses, it is irrelevant.) In four-ball match play, if a putt has been conceded but the player goes ahead and putts anyway because he hopes to show his partner the correct line, the *partner* should be disqualified from that hole, since he was the intended beneficiary of the act.

The first sentence of Rule 2-5 handles the everyday problem of what to do when opponents differ on a Rule or simply don't know the answer. They should continue play even though the status of the match is in doubt. The standing of the match is adjusted according to the ruling they receive later.

Focus on the word "claim" in Rule 2-5. It's synonymous with the more commonly used "call"—as in "I call this hole on you." Claims must be timely. If you see your opponent violate a Rule during the play of the second hole and that hole is halved or won by him, don't bother mentioning the violation during the play of the third hole. Too late. You can't hold your claim in reserve, and all you've done is create a chilled atmosphere.

On the other hand, if your opponent violated a Rule during the second hole and you weren't aware at the time but learned of the violation later, the clock hasn't run out on your right to claim. We'll get to that in Rule 34.

Violations generally call for loss of hole in match play. Exceptions to the general penalty are specified in certain Rules. An example occurs in Rule 18 when a player accidentally moves his ball. It's a one-stroke penalty, not loss of hole, and the ball must be replaced.

RULE 3

STROKE PLAY

The competitor who plays the stipulated round or rounds in the fewest strokes is the winner.

3-1
Winner

If a competitor fails to hole out at any hole and does not correct his mistake before he plays a stroke from the next teeing ground or, in the case of the last hole of the round, before he leaves the putting green, *he shall be disqualified.*

3-2
Failure to Hole Out

a. PROCEDURE
In stroke play only, when during play of a hole a competitor is doubtful of his rights or procedure, he may, without penalty, play a second ball. After the situation which caused the doubt has arisen, the competitor should, before taking further action, announce to his marker or a fellow-competitor his decision to invoke this Rule and the ball with which he will score if the Rules permit.

The competitor shall report the facts to the Committee before returning his score card unless he scores the same with both balls; if he fails to do so, *he shall be disqualified.*
b. DETERMINATION OF SCORE FOR HOLE
If the Rules allow the procedure selected in advance by the competitor, the score with the ball selected shall be his score for the hole.

If the competitor fails to announce in advance his decision to invoke this Rule or his selection, the score with the original ball or, if the original ball is not one of the the balls being played, the first ball put into play shall count if the Rules allow the procedure adopted for such ball.

3-3
Doubt as to Procedure

29

Note: A second ball played under Rule 3-3 is not a provisional ball under Rule 27-2.

3-4

Refusal to Comply with a Rule

If a competitor refuses to comply with a Rule affecting the rights of another competitor, *he shall be disqualified.*

3-5

General Penalty

The penalty for a breach of a Rule in stroke play is two strokes except when otherwise provided.

Stroke play is commonly called "medal play"—a term derived from the old British custom of playing occasional one-day competitions for the prize of a medal. (My permanent prize for winning the 1982 U.S. Open, by the way, is the USGA's gold medal.) Until the eighteenth century, when golf was already hundreds of years old, the game was always played at match play. Stroke play was inspired by the need for a means of completing a tournament in only one day.

Match play was still the preferred style of play when the USGA established its championships in 1895. The first U.S. Amateur was played at match play, and the next day the U.S. Open was tagged on almost as an afterthought at stroke play (thirty-six holes in one day so the ten competing pros wouldn't be away too long from their shops).

A classic application of Rule 3-2 occurred on the final hole of the playoff for the 1962 U.S. Open at Oakmont, near Pittsburgh. Jack Nicklaus, a twenty-one-year-old rookie pro, needed to hole a putt of only three feet for a 71. Jack had marked the position of his ball with a coin. Meanwhile, Arnold Palmer was lining up a longer putt, which he made for a 74. He then graciously picked up Jack's coin as an act of concession. Joseph C. Dey, Jr., former USGA executive director, immediately ordered Jack to replace the coin and hole out. You see, there is no such animal in stroke play as a concession. Technically, if Jack had walked off the 18th green without holing out, he could have been disqualified.

3-3. Doubt as to Procedure

The privilege of playing a second ball applies only in stroke play and not in match play. Why not in match play? Because the essence of match play is that players should know the status of the match. The introduction of a second ball erodes that right. The vital element of strategy in match play goes out the window if a player has to play against two balls, not knowing which one counts.

An application of Rule 3-3 might go like this: Your ball is embedded on a closely mown slope near a stream, but you don't know if the ball is within the hazard or not because the Committee has been remiss in its duty to define the margin of the hazard.

If the ball is within the hazard, you're out of luck. If it's outside the hazard, you're entitled to relief without penalty (see Rule 25-2). So tell your marker you are going to invoke this Rule, and don't forget to state the obvious—that you want the score with the *second* ball to count. If you don't, the score made with the original ball will count.

Then play both balls into the hole—the first under the premise that it was within the hazard and the second as if you were entitled to a free drop.

When you've finished the round, dump the case into the lap of the Committee. It's up to them to decide whether your original ball was within the hazard.

If it turns out that you make the same score with both balls you don't have to go to the Committee. That's a 1988 change. Previously, failure to report this situation meant disqualification.

3-4. Refusal to Comply with a Rule

Frankly, I've never seen an occasion when this Rule had to be applied. It could happen, I suppose, if a hardheaded player who thinks he knows the Rules refuses to lift his ball on the apron of a putting green when asked to do so by another player who is about to play on that line, a right granted in Rule 22. Hardhead is disqualified.

3-5. General Penalty

Violations in stroke play generally call for two strokes, but some transgressions call for disqualification. One example of the latter is practicing on the course itself on the day of a competition. An example of a one-stroke penalty occurs when a player, his partner or the caddie accidentally moves the player's ball.

CLUBS AND THE BALL

The United States Golf Association and the Royal and Ancient Golf Club of St. Andrew reserve the right to change the Rules and make and change the interpretations relating to clubs, balls and other implements at any time.

RULE 4

CLUBS

If there may be any reasonable basis for doubt as to whether a club which is to be manufactured conforms with Rule 4 and Appendix II,* the manufacturer should submit a sample to the United States Golf Association for a ruling, such sample to become its property for reference purposes. If a manufacturer fails to do so, he assumes the risk of a ruling that the club does not conform with the Rules of Golf.

A player in doubt as to the conformity of a club should consult the United States Golf Association.

4-1

Form and Make of Clubs

A club is an implement designed to be used for striking the ball.

A putter is a club designed primarily for use on the putting green.

The player's clubs shall conform with the provisions of this Rule and with the specifications and interpretations set forth in Appendix II.

a. GENERAL

The club shall be composed of a shaft and a head. All parts of the club shall be fixed so that the club is one unit. The club shall not be designed to be adjustable except for weight. The club shall not be substantially different from the traditional and customary form and make.

---

* Hereafter when in the text of the Rules themselves reference is made to Appendices, please note that these may be found in the USGA's *Rules of Golf* booklet.

b. SHAFT

The shaft shall be generally straight, with the same bending and twisting properties in any direction, and shall be attached to the clubhead at the heel either directly or through a single plain neck or socket. A putter shaft may be attached to any point in the head.

c. GRIP

The grip consists of that part of the shaft designed to be held by the player and any material added to it for the purpose of obtaining a firm hold. The grip shall be substantially straight and plain in form and shall not be molded for any part of the hands.

d. CLUBHEAD

The distance from the heel to the toe of the clubhead shall be greater than the distance from the face to the back. The clubhead shall be generally plain in shape.

The clubhead shall have only one face designed for striking the ball, except that a putter may have two such faces if their characteristics are the same, they are opposite each other and the loft of each is the same and does not exceed ten degrees.

e. CLUB FACE

The face shall not have any degree of concavity and, in relation to the ball, shall be hard and rigid. It shall be generally smooth except for such markings as are permitted by Appendix II. If the basic structural material of the head and face of a club, other than a putter, is metal, no inset or attachment is permitted.

f. WEAR

A club which conforms with Rule 4-1 when new is deemed to conform after wear through normal use. Any part of a club which has been purposely altered is regarded as new and must conform, in the altered state, with the Rules.

g. DAMAGE

If a player's club ceases to conform with Rule 4-1 because of damage sustained in the normal course of play, the player may:

(i) use the club in its damaged state, but only for the remainder of the <u>stipulated round</u> during which such damage was sustained; or

(ii) without unduly delaying play, repair it.

A club which ceases to conform because of damage sustained other than in the normal course of play shall not subsequently be used during the round.

(Damage changing playing characteristics of club—see Rule 4-2.)

During a <u>stipulated round</u>, the playing characteristics of a club shall not be purposely changed.

If the playing characteristics of a player's club are changed during a round because of damage sustained in the normal course of play, the player may:

4-2

Playing Characteristics Not to Be Changed

Illegal Clubs

Most of these clubs, for a variety of reasons, do not conform to the Rules of Golf. They're on display at the USGA Museum—open daily to the public without charge—at Far Hills, New Jersey. Incidentally, that piece of plumbing second from the bottom is actually a putter (one of many) sent to Arnold Palmer with the thought that it might cure his problems on the greens. Arnold lent many of the more imaginative gifts to the USGA. (R. 4)

(i) use the club in its altered state; or

(ii) without unduly delaying play, repair it.

If the playing characteristics of a player's club are changed because of damage sustained other than in the normal course of play, the club shall not subsequently be used during the round.

Damage to a club which occurred prior to a round may be repaired during the round, provided the playing characteristics are not changed and play is not unduly delayed.

4-3
Foreign Material

No foreign material shall be applied to the club face for the purpose of influencing the movement of the ball.

PENALTY FOR BREACH OF RULE 4-1, -2 OR -3:
Disqualification.

4-4
Maximum of Fourteen Clubs

a. SELECTION AND REPLACEMENT OF CLUBS

The player shall start a stipulated round with not more than fourteen clubs. He is limited to the clubs thus selected for that round except that, without unduly delaying play, he may:

(i) if he started with fewer than fourteen, add as many as will bring his total to that number; and

(ii) replace, with any club, a club which becomes unfit for play in the normal course of play.

b. BORROWING OR SHARING CLUBS

The addition or replacement of a club or clubs may be made by borrowing from anyone; only the borrower may use such club or clubs for the remainder of the round.

The sharing of a club or clubs is prohibited except that partners may share clubs, provided that the total number of clubs carried by the partners so sharing does not exceed fourteen.

PENALTY FOR BREACH OF RULE 4-4a OR b,
REGARDLESS OF NUMBER OF EXCESS CLUBS CARRIED:

Match play—At the conclusion of the hole at which the breach is discovered, the state of the match shall be adjusted by deducting one hole for each hole at which a breach occurred. Maximum deduction per round: two holes.

Stroke play—Two strokes for each hole at which any breach occurred; maximum penalty per round: four strokes.

Bogey and par competitions—Penalties as in match play.

Stableford competitions—See Note to Rule 32-1b.

c. EXCESS CLUB DECLARED OUT OF PLAY

Any club carried or used in breach of this Rule shall be declared out of play by the player immediately upon discovery that a breach has occurred and thereafter shall not be used by the player during the round.

PENALTY FOR BREACH OF RULE 4-4c: *Disqualification.*

Rules 4 and 5 exist in order to preserve the challenge of the game. Without reasonable standards, space-age technology might lead to new kinds of clubs and balls that would change the very nature of the game. An armaments race in golf makes no sense at all.

The USGA's annual budget for equipment testing and research is more than half a million dollars, money well spent.

4-1. Form and Make of Clubs

Sophisticated golfers who might worry about the grooves in their iron clubs becoming too wide through wear need not worry. Rule 4-1f affirms that the club remains legal so long as it was okay when new and it became worn from normal use.

4-2. Playing Characteristics Not to Be Changed

An example of a violation of this Rule would be the addition of lead tape to a driver *during* a round. It's all right to add or remove tape *before* a round.

4-3. Foreign Material

The prohibitions against applying "foreign material" to the club face or the ball are reactions against imaginative golfers who applied materials such as chalk or Vaseline in order, they claimed, to get more distance or to keep the ball on a straighter line by reducing spin. When I played on the Stanford University golf team, teammate Sandy Adelman spit on the face of his driver on every tee. That was before the USGA issued a Rules of Golf Decision on that very point. Sandy Adelman might not agree, but the USGA insists that "saliva is considered foreign material."

4-4. Maximum of Fourteen Clubs

There was no limit on the number of clubs until 1938. The ceiling was established because some players had gone to extremes in terms of carrying "specialty" clubs, supposedly designed to fit every kind of shot. Golf bags were becoming arsenals. Lawson Little and Craig Wood, two of the stars of the 1930s, went forth to battle with twenty-five clubs each. On the other hand, when Francis Ouimet won the 1913 U.S. Open, his ten-year-old caddie Eddie Lowery carried only seven clubs.

The number fourteen was selected as the maximum because it corresponded to what was generally thought to be a standard set of clubs. Most touring pros carry irons numbered 1 through 9, pitching and sand wedges, a putter and only two woods, although there has been a recent shift by some who add a third, very lofted, wedge. Something has to go—one of the irons.

Applying penalties for violations of Rule 4-4 can be tricky. Suppose in a match, player A is 2-up against B after sixteen holes. They discover on the 17th tee that A has been carrying fifteen clubs. The status of the match immediately becomes all square, since A gets the maximum penalty—loss of two holes.

Another example: A wins the first hole of a match against B, who then finds he's got an extra club. Poor B goes from 1 down to 2 down even though he's only played one hole, since the penalty is applied to the state of the match at the conclusion of the hole. Incidentally, they don't skip the second hole; the match resumes on the second tee with the penalty added.

There have been inadvertent and odd violations of Rule 4-4 on the tour. I was paired with Johnny Miller in the first round of the 1976 World Series of Golf when he suffered the maximum penalty of four strokes. As we were playing the 18th hole, Johnny noticed a tiny club in the bottom of his bag. It was an old Bull's-Eye putter he had modified for his son. In fact it was nothing but grip and head, about eighteen inches long. Nevertheless, it was a golf club and it changed Johnny's 72 into a 76. Unfair? Not necessarily. As a matter of fact, I often play with a friend who crouches over a putter that's not much longer than the one Johnny cut down for his son.

Just about every player I know has carried an extra club or more at some time. It happened to me once—in a qualifying round for the Missouri Amateur Championship. I managed to go out with eighteen clubs. At that time the penalty called for a maximum of four penalty strokes for every extra club. My 76 was converted into a nifty 92. That's the last time I or my caddie forgot to count my clubs before starting a round.

Iron Byron

There's no other machine quite like the USGA's Iron Byron, the USGA's mechanical golfer, which plays on a course all its own—a test range at USGA headquarters. The prototype was built to emulate the swing of my friend and mentor Byron Nelson. The USGA machine is rigged with a laser beam and high-speed photo equipment. Every hit is dissected to the extent of a recording of the speed of the club at impact (in millionths of a second) and wind velocity (both horizontally and vertically) during the six seconds the ball is in flight. During the USGA Overall Distance Standard tests, a ball is teed just after being removed from an incubator where it was stored at 75°F. When the clubhead strikes the ball, it will be moving at 109 miles per hour—about the clubhead speed of a long driver on the Tour.

I also stumbled all over Rule 4-4 at the 1986 Vantage Championship. There was a weather delay which meant I only finished 14 holes. That night I practiced with another putter. The next day, when play resumed on the 15th hole, my caddie, Bruce Edwards, noticed I had changed putters. Violation! You can't change clubs *during* a round if you start with 14.

Rule 4-4 limits you to the fourteen clubs you start with unless a club "becomes unfit for play in the normal course of play." When a shaft breaks as you're playing a stroke, you are entitled to a substitute, but you can't delay play. On the other hand, snapping a putter over your knee is not considered "in the normal course of play." Neither is a rap on the ground which causes an old shaft to break. That's what happened to Ben Crenshaw and his justly famous putter early in his match against Eamon Darcy in the 1987 Ryder Cup Match. Ben had to play on without a putter.

Millions of TV viewers saw Ray Floyd accidentally break the shaft of an iron club against a tree in the last round of the 1983 Tournament of Champions at La Costa. The incident happened on the last hole, so Raymond was not concerned about a replacement. But had it occurred, say, on the 9th hole, Raymond could have sent back into the pro shop or locker room for another club, and it could have been any club he desired—a wood or even a second putter—to bring his total up to fourteen.

RULE 5

THE BALL

5-1
General

The ball the player uses shall conform to specifications set forth in Appendix III on maximum weight, minimum size, spherical symmetry, initial velocity and overall distance when tested under specified conditions.

5-2
Foreign Material

No foreign material shall be applied to a ball for the purpose of changing its playing characteristics.

PENALTY FOR BREACH OF RULE 5-1 OR -2:
Disqualification.

5-3
Ball Unfit for Play

A ball is unfit for play if it is visibly cut, cracked or out of shape. A ball is not unfit for play solely because mud or other materials adhere to it, its surface is scratched or scraped or its paint is damaged or discolored.

If a player has reason to believe his ball has become unfit for play during play of the hole being played, he may during the play of such hole lift his ball without penalty to determine whether it is unfit, provided he announces his intention in advance to his opponent in match play or his marker or a fellow-competitor in stroke play and gives his opponent, marker or fellow-competitor an opportunity to examine the ball. If he lifts the ball without announcing his intention in advance or giving his opponent, marker or fellow-competitor an opportunity to examine the ball, *he shall incur a penalty of one stroke.*

⸍If it is determined that the ball has become unfit for play during play of the hole being played, the player may substitute another ball, placing it on the spot where the original ball lay. Otherwise, the original ball shall be replaced.

If a ball breaks into pieces as a result of a stroke, the stroke shall be replayed without penalty (see Rule 20-5).

*PENALTY FOR BREACH OF RULE 5-3:

Match play—Loss of hole; Stroke play—Two strokes.

Note 1: *The ball may not be cleaned to determine whether it is unfit for play—see Rule 21.*

Note 2: *If the opponent, marker or fellow-competitor wishes to dispute a claim of unfitness, he must do so before the player plays another ball.*

An historic difference between the USGA and the R&A Rules of Golf will come to an end on January 1, 1990, when the R&A will adopt the 1.68-inch ball. Thus, the Rules of Golf will be the same in all respects the world over. The R&A had allowed balls not less than 1.62 inches in diameter. A ball that size was called "a small ball."

Not long ago a spate of mail-order magazine ads appeared for unnamed brands of balls, promising extra distance, and alerting, or teasing, the reader to the truth that the ball is not approved by the USGA. The kicker "for tournament play" was sometimes appended. Some of these balls are nothing more than 1.62-inch balls. It's true they don't conform to USGA Rules, but almost all golfers rely on the Rules of Golf in everyday play and not just in competitions. A score made with a 1.62-inch ball can't be turned in for USGA handicap purposes either.

5-3. Ball Unfit for Play

Rule 5-3 begins with a commonsense definition of "unfit for play." An opponent, marker or fellow-competitor has the right to question a judgment that a ball is unfit for play.

The 1988 Rules close what I feel was a loophole. A player whose ball was scraped used to be able to declare it unfit for play on the basis that its true flight or roll could be affected. Now the ball has to be visibly cut, cracked or out of shape to qualify as unfit for play. Scratches and scrapes, despite the technical argument that they affect a ball's performance, are not grounds for declaring a ball unfit for play.

The advent of balls with plastic cores and of one-piece balls prompted the Rulesmakers to establish that when a ball breaks into pieces, the stroke is canceled.

I'm finicky about the balls I use on the tour. Most of us put a brand-new ball into play on every fourth hole. Moreover, I won't use a ball on a subsequent hole after I've scarred it playing a bunker shot. I probably average eight balls a round.

---

* If a player incurs the general penalty for breach of Rule 5-3, no additional penalty under the Rule shall be applied.

PLAYER'S RESPONSIBILITIES

RULE 6

THE PLAYER

DEFINITION

A "marker" is one who is appointed by the Committee to record a competitor's score in stroke play. He may be a fellow-competitor. He is not a referee.

6-1
Conditions of Competition

The player is responsible for knowing the conditions under which the competition is to be played (Rule 33-1).

6-2
Handicap

a. MATCH PLAY

Before starting a match in a handicap competition, the players should determine from one another their respective handicaps. If a player begins the match having declared a higher handicap which would affect the number of strokes given or received, *he shall be disqualified;* otherwise, the player shall play off the declared handicap.

b. STROKE PLAY

In any round of a handicap competition, the competitor shall ensure that his handicap is recorded on his score card before it is returned to the Committee. If no handicap is recorded on his score card before it is returned, or if the recorded handicap is higher than that to which he is entitled and this affects the number of strokes received, *he shall be disqualified* from that round of the handicap competition; otherwise, the score shall stand.

Note: *It is the player's responsibility to know the holes at which handicap strokes are to be given or received.*

a. TIME OF STARTING

The player shall start at the time laid down by the Committee.

b. GROUPS

In stroke play, the competitor shall remain throughout the round in the group arranged by the Committee unless the Committee authorizes or ratifies a change.

PENALTY FOR BREACH OF RULE 6-3: *Disqualification.*

(Best-ball and four-ball play—see Rules 30-3a and 31-2.)

Note: *The Committee may provide in the conditions of a competition (Rule 33-1) that, if the player arrives at his starting point, ready to play, within five minutes after his starting time, in the absence of circumstances which warrant waiving the penalty of disqualification as provided in Rule 33-7, the penalty for failure to start on time is loss of the first hole in match play or two strokes at the first hole in stroke play instead of disqualification.*

6-3
Time of Starting and Groups

The player may have only one caddie at any one time, *under penalty of disqualification.*

For any breach of a Rule by his caddie, the player incurs the applicable penalty.

6-4
Caddie

The responsibility for playing the proper ball rests with the player. Each player should put an identification mark on his ball.

6-5
Ball

a. RECORDING SCORES

After each hole the marker should check the score with the competitor and record it. On completion of the round the marker shall sign the card and hand it to the competitor. If more than one marker records the scores, each shall sign for the part for which he is responsible.

b. SIGNING AND RETURNING CARD

After completion of the round, the competitor should check his score for each hole and settle any doubtful points with the Committee. He shall ensure that the marker has signed the card, countersign the card himself and return it to the Committee as soon as possible.

PENALTY FOR BREACH OF RULE 6-6b: *Disqualification.*

c. ALTERATION OF CARD

No alteration may be made on a card after the competitor has returned it to the Committee.

d. WRONG SCORE FOR HOLE

The competitor is responsible for the correctness of the score recorded for each hole. If he returns a score for any hole lower than actually taken, *he shall be disqualified.* If he returns a score for any hole higher than actually taken, the score as returned shall stand.

Note 1: *The Committee is responsible for the addition of*

6-6
Scoring in Stroke Play

41

scores and application of the handicap recorded on the card —see Rule 33-5.

Note 2: *In four-ball stroke play, see also Rule 31-4 and -7a.*

6-7
Undue Delay

The player shall play without undue delay. Between completion of a hole and playing from the next teeing ground, the player shall not unduly delay play.

PENALTY FOR BREACH OF RULE 6-7:

Match play—Loss of hole; Stroke play—Two strokes. For repeated offense—Disqualification.

If the player unduly delays play between holes, he is delaying the play of the next hole and the penalty applies to that hole.

6-8
Discontinuance of Play

a. WHEN PERMITTED

The player shall not discontinue play unless:

(i) the Committee has suspended play;

(ii) he believes there is danger from lightning;

(iii) he is seeking a decision from the Committee on a doubtful or disputed point (see Rules 2-5 and 34-3); or

(iv) there is some other good reason, such as sudden illness.

Bad weather is not of itself a good reason for discontinuing play.

If the player discontinues play without specific permission from the Committee, he shall report to the Committee as soon as practicable. If he does so and the Committee considers his reason satisfactory, the player incurs no penalty. Otherwise, *the player shall be disqualified.*

Exception in match play: Players discontinuing match play by agreement are not subject to disqualification unless by so doing the competition is delayed.

Note: *Leaving the course does not of itself constitute discontinuance of play.*

b. PROCEDURE WHEN PLAY SUSPENDED BY COMMITTEE

When play is suspended by the Committee, if the players in a match or group are between the play of two holes, they shall not resume play until the Committee has ordered a resumption of play. If they are in the process of playing a hole, they may continue provided they do so without delay. If they choose to continue, they shall discontinue either before or immediately after completing the hole, and shall not thereafter resume play until the Committee has ordered a resumption of play.

PENALTY FOR BREACH OF RULE 6-8b: *Disqualification.*

c. LIFTING BALL WHEN PLAY DISCONTINUED

When during the play of a hole a player discontinues play under Rule 6-8a, he may lift his ball. A ball may be cleaned when so lifted. If a ball has been so lifted, the player shall, when play is resumed, place a ball on the spot from which the original ball was lifted.

> ## PENALTY FOR BREACH OF RULE 6-8c:
> *Match play—Loss of hole; Stroke play—Two strokes.*

Rule 6 contains a potpourri of items that have nothing to do with striking the ball, or with where it goes, but which nonetheless are essential to orderly and sound procedure. The provisions of Rule 6 underscore the principle that golf is a game that can endure only if the players act responsibly.

6-1. Conditions of Competition

Golf administrators use the phrase "conditions of play." These include the essentials: form of play (match or stroke, individual or team); whether or not it's a handicap event, and if so, what form; who is eligible; the dates and the starting times; whether there's an entry fee; and the prizes. It's up to the player to learn the conditions.

6-2. Handicap

The imperative word *shall* is used to require match play opponents to inform each other of their handicaps before play begins.

The advent of Slope in the USGA Handicap System makes handicapping fairer but it also requires an extra step by the golfer to know the correct number of handicap strokes. First, there is the matter of the Handicap Index, expressed in a decimal, *e.g.,* 11.8. Next, the golfer has to go to the Slope chart for his course to convert the Handicap Index into strokes received. An 11.8 might receive 13 or 14 strokes on a high Slope course; or the number of strokes might drop to 10 on a low Slope course.

The USGA Handicap System—which is nationally accepted—recommends that current handicaps be used for each round. In a handicap competition played over a period of weeks, the handicaps can go up or down with each revision.

In stroke play competitions, there is a strict provision that the handicaps in effect for each round be noted on the score cards returned to the Committee.

6-3. Time of Starting and Groups

One of the most publicized instances of a player missing his starting time came in the 1980 U.S. Open at Baltusrol, when Seve Ballesteros rushed to the first tee—too late.

A Committee will waive the disqualification penalty for good reason. Example? You're trapped for hours in a motel elevator. But running out of gas, getting lost or your alarm failing to work are examples of personal snafus that will not cut it with Committees.

6-4. Caddie

A player and his caddie are an integral and intimate unit, and they share responsibility for upholding the Rules. For example, if a caddie steps on a scuff mark on the player's line of putt, the player is penalized.

My regular tour caddie is Bruce Edwards. I trust him implicitly. Bruce has never cost me a penalty stroke.

Touring pro Jodie Mudd was less fortunate at the 1983 Heritage

Classic. Jodie was near the lead in the midst of his second round when we had an interruption of play because of bad weather. When the signal was given to resume play, Jodie returned to the course promptly, but his caddie, who had Jodie's clubs, was late in getting there. Jodie was disqualified.

6-5. Ball

The Rules, in this instance, use the word "should" rather than "shall," so it's not a violation if you don't put a distinctive mark on your ball. But suppose you're playing Brand X, with a number 1 on it, and you yank your drive into the rough. When you get to the likely spot, you find two Brand X number 1s. What you've got on your hands is a lost ball—unless you can with certainty identify your ball. My identifying marks are a couple of pencil-point marks in the dimple on the right of the number on each ball.

6-6. Scoring in Stroke Play

These provisions are limited to stroke play because scoring in match play depends entirely on the opponents' agreement or under-standing as to the status of the match. It's wise to keep a score card during a match, but the card itself has no official status and it need not be signed or turned in. You need only present the result to the Committee.

As for stroke play, the application of Rule 6-6 has prompted some of the most celebrated Rules controversies in the history of the game. Roberto De Vicenzo should have tied Bob Goalby for first in the 1968 Masters and played off the next day, but Roberto, who had made a birdie 3 on the 17th hole, countersigned the card prepared by Tommy Aaron, his marker, which erroneously showed 4 in the box for the 17th hole. According to Rule 6-6, the higher score had to stand, and the one-stroke difference made Roberto the runner-up.

Back in 1957, a similarly unhappy incident involved Jackie Pung. She was disqualified from the Women's Open Championship because she countersigned a card that had her making a 5 at the 4th hole, where she had actually made a 6. The total on the card was correct. A simple error of transposition had been made by her marker. Mrs. Pung's card should have read "5–6" for two successive holes, but instead it read "6–5."

Personally, I'll take Rule 6-6 just the way it is. It gives me the absolute right to be responsible for my score. I don't have to sign the card until and unless I'm satisfied with what it shows. Any alteration would erode that privilege.

The marker in tour events is always another player in the same group. A scorer accompanies each group. The card the scorer maintains is the source of scores for the scoreboards and the media. As soon as I finish, I always double-check my score card by first circling and checking my birdies and bogeys and then going over the card hole by hole with the unofficial scorer.

Actually, the most common cause for disqualification under Rule 6-6 is forgetting to sign the card. That's the first and last thing I think about in the scoring tent. So far I've never been disqualified for turning in an incorrect card or failing to sign one.

6-7. Undue Delay

In my view, golf has been allowed to become too slow a game, and I tend to think golf associations, including both the USGA and the PGA Tour, have been too lenient about imposing penalties for slow play.

6-8. Discontinuance of Play

Discontinuing play, the subject of Rule 6-8, is often a touchy question in club match play when one player or team wants to stop and the other wants to continue. Let's assume it's raining hard but that the course remains eminently playable. If a Committee has not suspended play in a storm *without* lightning, the side that wants to forge on has the right to do so. But note the General Exception to the effect that in match play opponents can by mutual agreement suspend play, provided that they don't cause the competition to be delayed.

Lightning is, of course, bad news. Rule 6-8 gives any player the right to stop when "he believes there is danger from lightning." He doesn't have to consult with his opponents, fellow-competitors or the Committee.

During the 1975 Western Open, Lee Trevino, Jerry Heard and Bobby Nichols were all hurt when a bolt of lightning struck near their improvised shelter from the storm while play was suspended. Every year golfers are killed by lightning, and it's impossible to be overly cautious. When I saw a flash during the fourth round of the 1983 Open at Oakmont, I stopped immediately, even though my ball was on the 15th green, thirty feet from the hole. I marked my ball and took off. The USGA siren sounded a few seconds later. The next morning, when play resumed, I had the unique and unwanted experience of beginning play with a long, slick putt.

The USGA issues a poster on protection from lightning storms that should be prominently displayed in every locker room.

RULE 7

PRACTICE

7-1

Before or Between Rounds

a. MATCH PLAY

On any day of a match play competition, a player may practice on the competition <u>course</u> before a round.

b. STROKE PLAY

On any day of a stroke competition or play-off, a competitor shall not practice on the competition <u>course</u> or test the surface of any putting green on the course before a round or play-off. When two or more rounds of a stroke completion are to be played over consecutive days, practice between those rounds on any competition course remaining to be played is prohibited.

Exception: Practice putting or chipping on or near the first <u>teeing ground</u> before starting a round or play-off is permitted.

PENALTY FOR BREACH OF RULE 7-1b: *Disqualification.*

Note: *The Committee may in the conditions of a competi-*

tion (Rule 33-1) prohibit practice on the competition course on any day of a match play competition or permit practice on the competition course or part of the course (Rule 33-2c) on any day of or between rounds of a stroke competition.

7-2

During Round

A player shall not play a practice <u>stroke</u> either during the play of a hole or between the play of two holes except that, between the play of two holes, the player may practice putting or chipping on or near the <u>putting green</u> of the hole last played, any practice putting green or the <u>teeing ground</u> of the next hole to be played in the round, provided such practice stroke is not played from a hazard and does not unduly delay play (Rule 6-7).

Exception: When play has been suspended by the Committee, a player may, prior to resumption of play, practice (a) as provided in this Rule, (b) anywhere other than on the competition course and (c) as otherwise permitted by the Committee.

PENALTY FOR BREACH OF RULE 7-2:

Match play—Loss of hole; Stroke play—Two strokes.

In the event of a breach between the play of two holes, the penalty applies to the next hole.

Note 1: *A practice swing is not a practice <u>stroke</u> and may be taken at any place, provided the player does not breach the Rules.*

Note 2: *The Committee may prohibit practice on or near the <u>putting green</u> of the hole last played.*

The language of Rule 7 is finicky—and well it might be, since golf is an exercise in finite judgments and muscle memory skills. If you could rehearse each shot before playing it, golf would be a different and easier game. I've averaged a fraction more than 70 strokes a round on the tour. If the Rules allowed me to practice each shot one time before it counted, I think I could reduce that average to 66.

7-1. Before or Between Rounds

The restrictions against practicing on the course are markedly different in the two basic forms of play.

In match play, you are not prohibited from practicing on the course prior to a round. But in stroke play you are. Why? Opponents in a match obviously start at the same time and therefore have the same opportunity to go out and try some or all of the course in advance. But in stroke play, those with early starting times would not have the same opportunity to practice on-course as those with later times.

The Rule, however, gives the Committee the option of flopping both conditions. That is, practice on the course in match play may be banned and, conversely, may be allowed in stroke play. When that happens, it's up to the Committee to notify the players in the form of a condition of the competition.

Watch out for Rule 7-1 when you're involved in a 36-hole stroke play qualifying event. You may play the first round Saturday morning and decide to go on the course Saturday afternoon for some practice.

Don't! The penalty is disqualification unless the Committee specifically has said otherwise.

7-2. During Round

The wording of Rule 7-2 allows for such innocuous acts as chipping near or on a tee when you're delayed. It also permits you to practice-putt (or chip) on the hole you've just completed—assuming you don't play from a hazard and can do so without delaying play. On the pro tour, putting practice is prohibited, as Note 2 contemplates, because it might delay play. Besides, all that extra traffic in the critical area near the hole would roughen the surface to the detriment of those who have late starting times.

The application of the penalty for a violation of Rule 7-2 is curious. Suppose a player replays a bunker shot on the 4th hole, which he's just won in a match. That's a clear-cut violation, since he's played a practice stroke in a hazard, but which hole does he lose? The penalty applies to the *next* hole, which means that he and his opponent skip hole 5 entirely and proceed directly to the 6th tee.

The Rules of Golf Committee is often forced to weave its way through thickets of technicalities in interpreting the Rules. Here are four examples under the practice category:

● A man habitually tossed down plastic balls and hit them in the direction of the hole. His opponents complained bitterly. The player said swatting at plastic balls was not covered in the Rules of Golf. The USGA ruled that the player was in fact playing practice strokes in violation of Rule 7-2.

● A letter described a driving range adjacent to a fairway, and how a woman, after playing her second shot to the green, flicked a ball with a red band painted on it back to where it belonged on a practice range. This happened during stroke play, and the Committee socked her with two strokes. She took her case to the USGA, which ordained that "casually flicking a range ball, apparently only for the purpose of tidying up the course, should not be considered a violation." The Decision carefully pointed out that "under some circumstances" hitting a range ball back to the range would be a violation. Suppose the next shot calls for a carry of 190 yards over water, and the player carefully addresses a range ball with a 3-wood and bashes it back toward the practice tee.

● Then there is the notorious case of two prominent professionals, who shall not be named, who got out of sorts with each other. Player A, celebrated for his desire to play fast, was impatient with the group ahead and drove his ball before all three ahead played their second shots. Whereupon Player B addressed A's ball in the fairway and slammed it back at A, some 230 yards away, on the tee. The USGA ruled that B's act did not constitute practice but that it most certainly constituted a breach in accepted decorum and that in equity the Committee should impose the general penalty of two strokes.

● Just before the start of a stroke play round a player walked up to the front of the first tee and drove a ball over a fence out of bounds in order to get limbered up. That was a violation. So, by the way, is putting a ball dropped in a fairway while you are waiting for the group ahead to clear a green.

RULE 8

ADVICE; INDICATING LINE OF PLAY

Definition

"Advice" is any counsel or suggestion which could influence a player in determining his play, the choice of a club or the method of making a <u>stroke</u>.

Information on the Rules or on matters of public information, such as the position of hazards or the flagstick on the putting green, is not advice.

8-1

Advice

A player shall not give advice to anyone in the competition except his partner. A player may ask for advice from only his partner or either of their caddies.

8-2

Indicating Line of Play

a. OTHER THAN ON PUTTING GREEN

Except on the <u>putting green</u>, a player may have the line of play indicated to him by anyone, but no one shall stand on or close to the line while the <u>stroke</u> is being played. Any mark placed during the play of a hole by the player or with his knowledge to indicate the line shall be removed before the stroke is played.

Exception: Flagstick attended or held up—see Rule 17-1.

b. ON THE PUTTING GREEN

When the player's ball is on the <u>putting green</u>, the player, his partner or either of their caddies may, before but not during the <u>stroke</u>, point out a line for putting, but in so doing the putting green shall not be touched. No mark shall be placed anywhere to indicate a line for putting.

PENALTY FOR BREACH OF RULE:

Match play—Loss of hole; Stroke play—Two strokes.

Note: *In a team competition without concurrent individual competition, the Committee may in the conditions of the competition (Rule 33-1) permit each team to appoint one person, e.g., team captain or coach, who may give advice (including pointing out a line for putting) to members of that team. Such person shall be identified to the Committee prior to the start of the competition.*

8-1. Advice

I seem to be allergic to the advice Rule. During the 1968 Amateur Championship at the Scioto Country Club in Columbus, Ohio, I was paired with Mike Taylor, another young amateur, from Mississippi. We hit if off well. On one hole I yelled clear across a fairway to ask Mike what he'd hit, and he answered. USGA official Pete Tufts could hardly believe his ears. Mike and I were each penalized two strokes—I for asking for advice, and Mike for giving it.

Then, twelve years later, I was cruising with a big lead in the last round of the 1980 Tournament of Champions. I was paired with Lee Trevino, who was struggling that day. I noticed a little swing flaw Lee seemed to have picked up and told him about it.

Bob Goalby, working as a roving announcer for NBC, heard of our exchange and commented on it as an illustration of the kind of good feeling that exists on the tour—not as a violation of the Rules.

Plenty of TV viewers, however, pounced on Goalby's remark and called both NBC and the club. When I finished the round, but before I signed my score card, tour official Jack Tuthill told me about the calls and asked if I'd given Trevino advice. I said I had. Jack said, "Add 2 strokes." Thank goodness I had a 3-stroke lead. Since he had not asked for advice, Trevino wasn't penalized.

Some landmark interpretations of Rule 8:

• A player in a college match had a delicate 40-yard pitch shot to execute. He approved and watched with great interest as a teammate, at that point a spectator following the match, dropped a ball and played the shot. His opponent protested vehemently. The player, who may well have benefited from his teammate's action, should have lost the hole if he did not try to stop such an irregular procedure.

• A player wanted to take a lesson between rounds of a 36-hole match for his club championship. That's okay, because the ban against receiving advice applies only during the stipulated round, which consists of 18 holes. As a matter of fact, Jerry Pate skipped lunch between rounds of the final match of the 1974 U.S. Amateur, which he won, in order to take a lesson from Conrad Rehling, his college coach.

• A double caddie often finds himself in a delicate position. Player A asks their caddie what club player B, his opponent, just hit. It's no violation, because the definition of "caddie" told us that a double caddie "is always deemed to be the caddie of the player whose ball is involved." Since it was his ball that was involved, player A was entitled to attempt to pry loose any useful information the caddie possessed.

A golfer may, of course, ask his caddie for advice. He can also seek help from his partner or his partner's caddie. A partner, remember, is someone on your side. Neither Mike Taylor nor Lee Trevino was my partner; we were fellow-competitors.

A Committee in charge of a team event may allow team captains or coaches to give advice. If the Committee so authorizes, a college or high school coach can stand on the tee of a par-3 hole and tell his team members what clubs have been used on the hole earlier and by whom.

However, this is not allowable if the tournament honors an individual winner as well as the winning team.

The USGA has been forced to split some fine hairs in interpreting "advice." Asking an opponent or fellow-competitor to name the club he has used is forbidden, but it's not a violation if you *look* into his bag to discover which club is missing. On the other hand, if your opponent or fellow-competitor should go to the extreme of draping a towel over his clubs to maintain secrecy, you are not allowed to strip the towel. A Decision says so. (As a practical matter, if I'm close to another player, I can identify the club he's selected by the club face angle 90 percent of the time.)

The Rulesmakers also had to agonize over the modern vogue for playing the game by yardage numbers. I know how far from the hole I am before I play almost every shot, and I also know the location of

Brave the Elements
*The Rules do not permit
what's happening here. A
player cannot be shielded
from the elements in the act
of making a stroke. (R. 14-2)*

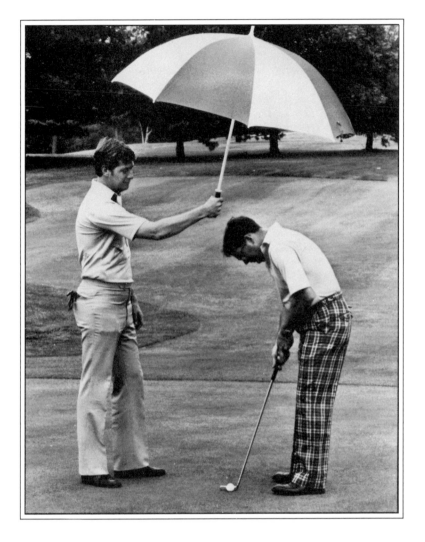

the hole on the green, which is expressed, for example, as six paces
from the front and five paces from the right on a chart produced by
tour officials and distributed at the first tee on each day of a tournament.

Given this availability of precise yardage data, what should happen
under the Rules when a player asks another about yardage or the
location of the hole, whether or not printed charts are available? Is
that asking for "advice" or isn't it? A Decision says that distance from
a tree, bunker or sprinkler head to the middle of the green is an
ascertainable fact, that the location of the hole is a matter of "public
information" and that neither comes under the heading of "counsel or
suggestion," which are defined as "advice."

But watch out for another Decision which says that if you ask for
distance information related to your ball—a non-permanent object—
you are asking for advice, in violation of Rule 8, on the grounds that
such information is not public. For what it's worth, I don't happen to

agree with this interpretation, but my disagreement is not relevant. What does matter is that there is a Decision on this fine point and that it be applied consistently.

A piece of obscure but interesting history: The practice of charting courses by yards in terms of reference points ("123 yards from front of fairway bunker on right to middle of green") was the product of the nimble mind of Gene Andrews, a first-class amateur from Southern California who won both the USGA Public Links and Senior Amateur Championships. Andrews first charted a treeless links course in Great Britain during a practice round before a 1950s British Amateur Championship because he found that the barren land allowed him no sense of distance. Andrews continued the practice at home. Deane Beman picked it up from Gene during the 1958 U.S. Amateur Championship and passed it along to his good friend Jack Nicklaus. It wasn't very long before the televised image of Nicklaus peering at his yardage notes in fairways aroused the curiosity, and mimicry, of golfers everywhere.

8-2. Indicating Line of Play

Rule 8-2a is simple enough. When you can't see what you're aiming at, anyone can help you out by indicating the line to the target. But before you play the stroke, your helper has to get off that line, although the flagstick *can* be held aloft to indicate the position of the hole.

The line of play on a putting green, however, is sacrosanct. Rule 8-2b is commonly violated when caddies or partners touch the green itself with a club or flagstick while pointing to what they consider to be the line. (The line, by the way, is not necessarily a straight line from ball to hole. The slope of the ground must be considered in resolving any questions about defining the line.)

RULE 9

INFORMATION AS TO STROKES TAKEN

The number of strokes a player has taken shall include any penalty strokes incurred.

9-1
General

A player who has incurred a penalty shall inform his opponent as soon as practicable. If he fails to do so, he shall be deemed to have given wrong information, even if he was not aware that he had incurred a penalty.

An opponent is entitled to ascertain from the player, during the play of a hole, the number of strokes he has taken and, after play of a hole, the number of strokes taken on the hole just completed.

If during the play of a hole the player gives or is deemed to give wrong information as to the number of strokes taken, he shall incur no penalty if he corrects the mistake before his

9-2
Match Play

opponent has played his next stroke. If the player fails so to correct the wrong information, *he shall lose the hole.*

If after play of a hole the player gives or is deemed to give wrong information as to the number of strokes taken on the hole just completed and this affects the opponent's understanding of the result of the hole, he shall incur no penalty if he corrects his mistake before any player plays from the next teeing ground or, in the case of the last hole of the match, before all players leave the putting green. If the player fails so to correct the wrong information, *he shall lose the hole.*

Indicating Line of Play

My caddie, or for that matter anyone else, can show me the line (left) *to the hole, but he isn't allowed to stand on or near the line while the stroke is being played. He's moved off the line in the picture at right. (R. 8-2)*

A competitor who has incurred a penalty should inform his marker as soon as practicable.

Rule 9 doesn't cause a stir in stroke play, since it all comes out in the wash at the end of a round when we check our cards, hole by hole. Rule 9-3 says that in stroke play a competitor should tell his marker of any penalties as soon as possible, but the difference between the conditional "should" and the absolute "shall" means that a competitor whose ball moves after he's taken his stance and addressed it need not shout that doleful fact to his marker, fifty yards on the other side of the fairway.

In match play, however, opponents should know how they stand at all times. If your opponent lies 3 in a bunker near the green, and you lie 1 only 125 yards from the hole, your next stroke is likely to be properly cautious. But if you think he only lies 2 because you don't know he incurred a penalty stroke along the way, you might be misled into flirting with the bunker yourself.

The word "deemed" in Rule 9 gives some readers pause. In this context, it means that a failure to announce that you've incurred a penalty is the same as being asked how many strokes you've taken and coming up with the wrong answer.

Here's an example of how wrong information applies to an act of omission: a player thinks he won the 5th hole but during the play of the 6th hole learns he played a wrong ball on the 5th. At that point the opponent's belated claim should be honored and the result of the match adjusted accordingly. The player failed to inform his opponent of a penalty (wrong ball) he incurred, even though he was not aware of it at the time (5th hole).

Note, by the way, that ignorance of the Rules is no excuse. Example: your opponent removes a leaf behind his ball in a bunker on the 9th hole, but you don't see that violation. The hole is then seemingly won by him. As you're strolling down the 10th fairway, he casually remarks that he was able to make a good bunker shot on the 9th because he moved a leaf. If you know what you're doing, you'll tell him that a leaf is a loose impediment which can't be removed from a hazard, and that by not revealing the violation (even though he didn't know there was a violation) he gave you wrong information. He therefore lost the 9th hole. Instead of being 1 down, you're now 1 up.

ORDER OF PLAY

ORDER OF PLAY

10-1

Match Play

a. TEEING GROUND

The side entitled to play first from the <u>teeing ground</u> is said to have the "honor."

The side which shall have the honor at the first teeing ground shall be determined by the order of the draw. In the absence of a draw, the honor should be decided by lot.

The side which wins a hole shall take the honor at the next teeing ground. If a hole has been halved, the side which had the honor at the previous teeing ground shall retain it.

b. OTHER THAN ON TEEING GROUND

When the balls are in play, the ball farther from the hole shall be played first. If the balls are equidistant from the hole, the ball to be played first should be decided by lot.

Exception: Rule 30-3c (best-ball and four-ball match play).

c. PLAYING OUT OF TURN

If a player plays when his opponent should have played, the opponent may immediately require the player to cancel the stroke so played and play a ball in correct order, without penalty (see Rule 20-5).

10-2

Stroke Play

a. TEEING GROUND

The competitor entitled to play first from the <u>teeing ground</u> is said to have the "honor."

The competitor who shall have the honor at the first teeing ground shall be determined by the order of the draw. In the absence of a draw, the honor should be decided by lot.

The competitor with the lowest score at a hole shall take the honor at the next teeing ground. The competitor with the second lowest score shall play next and so on. If two or more competitors have the same score at a hole, they shall play

Nudged Off the Tee
There's no penalty when a ball falls or is knocked off a tee before a stroke. The ball may be teed again. Remember, there can be no stroke without intent. (R. 11-3)

from the next teeing ground in the same order as at the previous teeing ground.

b. OTHER THAN ON TEEING GROUND

When the balls are in play, the ball farthest from the hole shall be played first. If two or more balls are equidistant from the hole, the ball to be played first should be decided by lot.

Exceptions: Rules 22 (ball interfering with or assisting play) and 31-5 (four-ball stroke play).

c. PLAYING OUT OF TURN

If a competitor plays out of turn, no penalty is incurred and the ball shall be played as it lies. If, however, the Committee determines that competitors have agreed to play in an order other than that set forth in Clauses 2a and 2b of this Rule to give one of them an advantage, *they shall be disqualified.*

(Incorrect order of play in threesomes and foursomes stroke play—see Rule 29-3.)

10-3
Provisional Ball or Second Ball from Teeing Ground

If a player plays a <u>provisional ball</u> or a second ball from a <u>teeing ground</u>, he should do so after his opponent or fellow-competitor has played his first <u>stroke</u>. If a player plays a provisional ball or a second ball out of turn, Clauses 1c and 2c of this Rule shall apply.

10-4
Ball Moved in Measuring

If a ball is moved in measuring to determine which ball is farther from the hole, no penalty is incurred and the ball shall be replaced.

The principle expressed in Rule 10 is that the ball farther from the hole shall be played first. Here's a summary of what happens when a ball is played out of turn in the two most common forms of play:

● Match play: The opponent may immediately require the player to replay the stroke. If played from the tee, the ball may be re-teed; if played through the green or from a hazard, the ball to be replayed is dropped; if played on a putting green, the ball is replaced. No penalty. This applies to both an individual and a four-ball match.

● Stroke play: No penalty, and the ball is played as it lies—not played over. However, if there's a conspiracy in order to circumvent the Rule in order to give one player an advantage, the players involved are to be disqualified. One example would occur on a par-3 hole played in a heavy wind when a player tries to help a friend by playing out of turn so the friend can gauge the effect of the wind on his ball.

Everyday golf is played on a handicap basis and the honor is determined by the net scores of the preceding hole.

One of my favorite golf stories turns on a question of "honor." According to Joe Dey, the USGA granted a special exemption from qualifying for the 1941 U.S. Open to one Dr. Walter Ratto of Brazil for reasons that are still obscure. Dr. Ratto stepped to the first tee of the Colonial Country Club at Fort Worth and slammed his ball into a tree very near the tee. The ball caromed behind the tee. The young American pro with whom Dr. Ratto was paired then asked the doctor, "Is it now my honor or are you away?" Answer: The pro should have driven.

TEEING GROUND

RULE II

TEEING GROUND

The "teeing ground" is the starting place for the hole to be played. It is a rectangular area two club-lengths in depth, the front and the sides of which are defined by the outside limits of two tee-markers. A ball is outside the teeing ground when all of it lies outside the teeing ground.

Definition

In teeing, the ball may be placed on the ground, on an irregularity of surface created by the player on the ground or on a tee, sand or other substance in order to raise it off the ground.

A player may stand outside the teeing ground to play a ball within it.

II-1

Teeing

Before a player plays his first stroke with any ball from the teeing ground of the hole being played, the tee-markers are deemed to be fixed. In such circumstances, if the player moves or allows to be moved a tee-marker for the purpose of avoiding interference with his stance, the area of his intended swing or his line of play, *he shall incur the penalty for a breach of Rule 13-2.*

II-2

Tee-Markers

If a ball, when not in play, falls off a tee or is knocked off a tee by the player in addressing it, it may be re-teed without penalty, but if a stroke is made at the ball in these circumstances, whether the ball is moving or not, the stroke counts but no penalty is incurred.

II-3

Ball Falling Off Tee

a. MATCH PLAY

If a player, when starting a hole, plays a ball from outside the teeing ground, the opponent may immediately require the player to cancel the stroke so played and play a ball from within the teeing ground, without penalty.

II-4

Playing Outside Teeing Ground

57

b. STROKE PLAY

If a competitor, when starting a hole, plays a ball from outside the <u>teeing ground</u>, *he shall incur a penalty of two strokes* and shall then play a ball from within the teeing ground.

If the competitor plays a stroke from the next teeing ground without first correcting his mistake or, in the case of the last hole of the round, leaves the <u>putting green</u> without first declaring his intention to correct his mistake, *he shall be disqualified.*

Strokes played by a competitor from outside the teeing ground do not count in his score.

11-1. Teeing

Historical note: The wooden tee was not invented until the turn of the century and didn't come into common use until the 1920s. Before then, balls were commonly teed on tiny pyramids of wet sand, which was usually stored in buckets near each tee.

11-2. Tee-Markers

I've never known an instance when a golfer purposely teed his ball in front of the tee-markers, but it does happen occasionally and usually because the markers have been installed so carelessly that a line drawn between the front of the markers would not form a right angle with the line of play.

Vandalism is a lamentable fact of life which, in one of its milder forms, often results in the disappearance of tee-markers. What to do when the markers aren't there?

If only one marker is removed, a Committee can decide to accept the scores of players who teed off from what they judged to be the teeing ground, provided no advantage was gained. But if both markers have been removed the players may not estimate a teeing area unless there is strong evidence indicating where the markers were. Such evidence would be depressions in the ground or other marks indicating the markers' former location.

11-3. Ball Falling Off Tee

Whenever a ball falls off or is nudged accidentally from a tee, some joker has to say "That's one." It is not, because the definition of a stroke told us that there is no stroke unless the club moves forward and the player *intends* to strike the ball. The ball is not in play until a stroke is made. Rule 11-3 is necessary only to resolve the question of whether or not the ball can be teed again—and of course it can.

● The atmosphere must have been electric in a club match reported by a Massachusetts golfer. It led to a decision which goes like this: A teed her ball, addressed it and then missed it completely. A whiff! Then, after addressing the ball again, A nudged her ball from the tee. B said A was then shooting 3 and must play the ball where it lay even though it was still within the teeing ground. A vehemently claimed she could re-tee without penalty.

Answer: Poor A did lie 2. The whiff was one stroke. According to a Definition, A's ball was in play as soon as she made a stroke on the teeing ground. Therefore A's ball was in play as soon as she whiffed it and it was also in play when she accidentally moved it. Since she moved it after address, she incurred a one-stroke penalty and had to replace the ball on the tee, as required by Rule 18-2b.

I can't help but remember John Mahaffey completing his stroke as his ball was toppling from the tee on a hole at the Firestone Country Club. John's driver barely made contact with the ball, which dribbled only a few yards off the tee and into a rotten lie. John, whose sense of humor is one of the tour's redeeming features, later lamented what terrible luck he'd suffered in not missing the ball entirely so that it still would have been teed up.

11-4. Playing Outside Teeing Ground

A ball teed outside the teeing ground raises a nice question of ethics. In match play the opponent of the player whose ball is teed in the wrong place has every opportunity to use the Rules cruelly by requiring the shot to be replayed. That's not the way the game should be played. If I saw an opponent's ball teed ahead of the markers, I'd let him know about it and I'd expect him to do the same for me.

Playing from outside the teeing ground in stroke play calls for a two-stroke penalty. Failure to rectify the mistake before playing from the next tee results in disqualification. Suppose a player in stroke play plays from the wrong set of tee-markers or is unfamiliar with the course and begins to play a hole out of sequence. Let's say he then plays a second stroke before the error is brought to his attention. Rule 11-4 says that he must return to the correct set of markers and play the hole correctly. The stroke he plays from the correct markers is his third (not fifth), since the strokes he played starting at the wrong markers do not count and only the penalty strokes are added.

PLAYING THE BALL

SEARCHING FOR AND IDENTIFYING BALL

Definitions

A "hazard" is any <u>bunker</u> or <u>water hazard</u>.

A "bunker' is a <u>hazard</u> consisting of a prepared area of ground, often a hollow, from which turf or soil has been removed and replaced with sand or the like. Grass-covered ground bordering or within a bunker is not part of the bunker. The margin of a bunker extends vertically downwards, but not upwards.

A "water hazard" is any sea, lake, pond, river, ditch, surface drainage ditch or other open water course (whether or not containing water) and anything of a similar nature.

All ground or water within the margin of a water hazard is part of the water hazard. The margin of a water hazard extends vertically upwards and downwards. Stakes and lines defining the margins of water hazards are in the hazards.

12-1

Searching for Ball; Seeing Ball

In searching for his ball anywhere on the course, the player may touch or bend long grass, rushes, bushes, whins, heather or the like, but only to the extent necessary to find and identify it, provided that this does not improve the lie of the ball, the area of his intended swing or his line of play.

A player is not necessarily entitled to see his ball when playing a stroke.

In a <u>hazard</u>, if a ball is covered by <u>loose impediments</u> or sand, the player may remove by probing, raking or other means as much thereof as will enable him to see a part of the ball. If an excess is removed, no penalty is incurred and the ball shall be re-covered so that only a part of the ball is visible. If the ball is moved in such removal, no penalty is incurred; the ball shall be replaced and, if necessary, re-covered. As to removal of loose impediments outside a hazard, see Rule 23.

Buried in Sand

My ball is completely buried in the sand of a bunker. All I'm allowed to do is brush aside enough sand so that I can see a piece of the ball—but no more. It doesn't matter if I can't identify the ball, since there's no penalty for playing a wrong ball in a hazard. (R. 12-1).

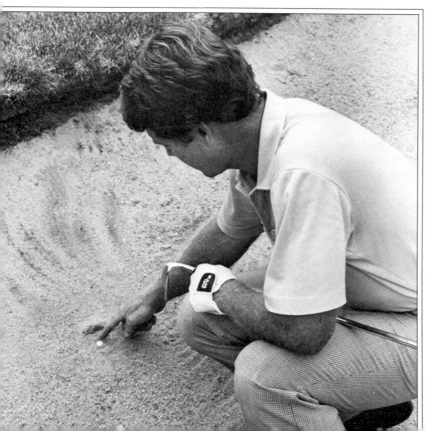

If a ball lying in <u>casual water</u>, <u>ground under repair</u> or a hole, cast or runway made by a burrowing animal, a reptile or a bird is accidentally moved during search, no penalty is incurred; the ball shall be replaced, unless the player elects to proceed under Rule 25-1b.

If a ball is believed to be lying in water in a <u>water hazard</u>, the player may probe for it with a club or otherwise. If the ball is moved in so doing, no penalty is incurred; the ball shall be replaced, unless the player elects to proceed under Rule 26-1.

PENALTY FOR BREACH OF RULE 12-1:
Match play—Loss of hole; Stroke play—Two strokes.

12-2
Identifying Ball

The responsibility for playing the proper ball rests with the player. Each player should put an identification mark on his ball.

Except in a <u>hazard</u>, the player may, without penalty, lift a ball he believes to be his own for the purpose of identification and clean it to the extent necessary for identification. If the ball is the player's ball, he shall replace it. Before the player lifts the ball, he shall announce his intention to his opponent in match play or his marker or a fellow-competitor in stroke play and give his opponent, marker or fellow-competitor an opportunity to observe the lifting and replacement. If he lifts his ball without announcing his intention in advance or giving his opponent, marker or fellow-competitor an opportunity to observe, or if he lifts his ball for identification in a hazard, *he shall incur a penalty of one stroke* and the ball shall be replaced.

If a player who is required to replace a ball fails to do so, *he shall incur the penalty* for a breach of Rule 20-3a, but no additional penalty under Rule 12-2 shall be applied.

12-1. Searching for Ball; Seeing Ball

A couple of key points:

• The need to identify a ball may not be used as an excuse to improve a lie. If a ball is lifted for identification from an awkward position, in heavy rough, it must be replaced in such a way that the subsequent stroke is just as difficult as if the ball was not lifted.

• A player who moves his ball accidentally while searching for it in casual water or ground under repair is not penalized as he would in searching for it through the green.

12-2. Identifying Ball

When a player isn't sure a ball is his, he must announce his intention to his opponent, marker or fellow-competitor, and give him the opportunity to observe the lifting and replacement. Incidentally, the position of the ball lifted must be marked—a requirement of Rule 20-1.

A ball lifted in this circumstance is *not* to be cleaned unless there's no other way to identify the ball, and then only enough to establish its identity.

The privilege of lifting for identification does not exist in hazards because there's no penalty for playing a wrong ball in a hazard.

RULE 13

BALL PLAYED AS IT LIES; AREA OF INTENDED SWING AND LINE OF PLAY; STANCE

A "hazard" is any <u>bunker</u> or <u>water hazard</u>.

A "bunker" is a <u>hazard</u> consisting of a prepared area of ground, often a hollow, from which turf or soil has been removed and replaced with sand or the like. Grass-covered ground bordering or within a bunker is not part of the bunker. The margin of a bunker extends vertically downwards, but not upwards.

A "water hazard" is any sea, lake, pond, river, ditch, surface drainage ditch or other open water course (whether or not containing water) and anything of a similar nature.

All ground or water within the margin of a water hazard is part of the water hazard. The margin of a water hazard extends vertically upwards and downwards. Stakes and lines defining the margins of water hazards are in the hazards.

Definitions

The ball shall be played as it lies, except as otherwise provided in the Rules.

(Ball at rest moved—see Rule 18.)

13-1

Ball Played As It Lies

Except as provided in the Rules, a player shall not improve or allow to be improved:

the position or lie of his ball,

the area of his intended swing,

his line of play or

the area in which he is to drop or place a ball by any of the following actions:

moving, bending or breaking anything growing or fixed (including immovable <u>obtructions</u> and objects defining <u>out of bounds</u>) or

removing or pressing down sand, loose soil, replaced divots, other cut turf placed in position or other irregularities of surface

except as follows:

as may occur in fairly taking his <u>stance</u>,

in making a <u>stroke</u> or the backward movement of his club for a stroke,

on the <u>teeing ground</u> in creating or eliminating irregularities of surface, or

on the <u>putting green</u> in removing sand and loose soil as provided in Rule 16-1a or in repairing damage as provided in Rule 16-1c.

13-2

Improving Lie, Area of Intended Swing or Line of Play

Don't Improve the Lie
Here's an example of a blatant violation. The lie is being improved by pressing down behind the ball so that it sits up better. One of the underlying principles behind the Rules of Golf is that you play the ball as it lies. (R. 13-2)

The club may be grounded only lightly and shall not be pressed on the ground.
Exception: Ball lying in or touching hazard—see Rule 13-4.

13-3
Building Stance

A player is entitled to place his feet firmly in taking his stance, but he shall not build a stance.

13-4
Ball Lying in or Touching a Hazard

Except as provided in the Rules, before making a <u>stroke</u> at a ball which lies in or touches a <u>hazard</u> (whether a <u>bunker</u> or a <u>water hazard</u>), the player shall not:

  a. Test the condition of the hazard or any similar hazard,

  b. Touch the ground in the hazard or water in the water hazard with a club or otherwise, or

  c. Touch or move a <u>loose impediment</u> lying in or touching the hazard.

Exceptions:

1. At address or in the backward movement for the stroke, the club may touch any <u>obstruction</u> or any grass, bush, tree or other growing thing.

2. The player may place his clubs in a <u>hazard</u>, provided nothing is done which may constitute testing the soil or improving the lie of the ball.

3. The player after playing the stroke, or his <u>caddie</u> at any time without the authority of the player, may smooth sand or soil in the hazard, provided that, if the ball still lies in the hazard, nothing is done which improves the lie of the ball or assists the player in his subsequent play of the hole.

PENALTY FOR BREACH OF RULE:
Match play—Loss of hole; Stroke play—Two strokes.

(Searching for ball—See Rule 12-1.)

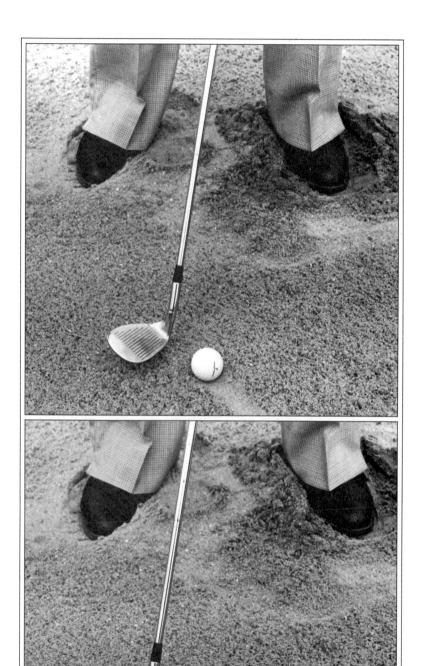

Touching a Hazard

Before you play a stroke in a hazard the ground (or, in a water hazard, the water) may not be touched. When a ball lies in a hazard, it is addressed as soon as the player takes a stance. If the club touches the sand during the backswing, there's a violation. (R. 13-4)

Grass in a Hazard

When a ball is playable in a water hazard it's often surrounded by tall grass. In the act of addressing the ball, I'm permitted to touch the grass, but it would be a violation to ground the club. (R. 13-4)

It may well be that Rule 13 is violated more often than any other Rule. The impulse to make the stroke a little bit easier by moving anything bothersome or by pressing down with the clubhead is powerful. Moreover, the application of this Rule often involves judgment rather than agreed-upon facts. This Rule is violated:

● When, during a practice swing, a branch or twig is snapped or leaves are removed and, as a result, the next stroke is easier to play.

● When a player brushes aside sand or loose soil on his line that is not on a putting green.

● When a ball lies in shrubbery and the player gets to the ball like a bull in a china shop by breaking, bending or moving branches that bother the stroke or were in his line and which he need not have disturbed in order to take a fair stance.

The R&A and USGA say this about the knocking down of leaves during a practice swing: "Whether a player who knocks leaves down with a practice swing is in breach of this Rule depends on the circumstances. In some cases the knocking down of a number of leaves would not improve the area of the intended swing, in which case there would be no breach of the Rules. In other cases, the knocking down of one large leaf might improve the area of the intended swing, in which case there would be a breach."

There was a famous violation of Rule 13-2 during the 1982 Tournament of Champions. Ron Streck, the leader, was inhibited by the branches of an evergreen tree as he addressed his ball. They obscured his vision. Ron braided the offending branches, which were right where he wanted his head to be. He had no idea he was wrong. But plenty of television viewers did. Their calls resulted in a review of the video tape before Ron completed his round. A two-stroke penalty was assessed.

TV viewers thought Andy Bean broke the same Rule during the 1982 Doral Tournament. Andy had knocked down a few leaves while practicing how to play a recovery shot next to a tree. It was ruled, and properly so, that the dislodging of those leaves did not assist him. Bean went on to win the tournament.

The words "line of play" seem to cry out for clarification. Hence this Decision explaining the term "line of play" in Rules 8-2, 13-2, 23-1 and 24-1: "The line of play is the direction which the player wishes his ball to take after a stroke plus a reasonable distance on either side of the intended direction and beyond the intended objective. The line of play is both in the air and on the ground."

Here's another "line of play" Decision: "There is a bunker between A's ball and the hole. Before playing, A smooths footprints and other irregularities in the bunker on his line of play. Was A in breach of Rule 13-2?"

"Yes, such action would improve the line of play, contrary to Rule 13-2."

As for Rule 13-3, an extreme example of "building a stance" would be to climb on a golf-cart seat to flail away at a ball lodged in a tree. A more common violation occurs when players, faced with taking an uneven stance in a bunker, pound down the side of a bunker with their heels in order to get their feet level.

I suppose the most famous "building a stance" ruling in the history of golf victimized Craig Stadler in the 1987 San Diego Open. During the third round the only way Craig could play a stroke was from his knees under the branches of a pine tree which was leaking sap. Before playing the stroke Craig put down a towel and kneeled on it. A Decision with exactly those sets of facts had recently been published. It held that such an act constitutes building a stance.

During the telecast of the fourth round NBC showed a tape of the towel incident. Neither the NBC producer nor Stadler had the slightest idea that the Rule had been violated. But a viewer did and placed a call that triggered application of the Rules which called for Craig to be DQ'd under Rule 6-6 since he had returned to a score for a hole lower than he'd actually taken during the third round.

There's some irony in this that Craig may not appreciate. The viewer mistakenly thought that the towel incident was live. He called not in the guise of a vengeful informer but with the hope that Stadler would

Ball Marks and Line of Play
You may repair a ball mark on the putting green (left) *even though your ball is off the putting green. But the right to repair ball marks is strictly*

limited to the putting green, so you may not repair a mark on your line on an apron (right) *even though you intend to putt. The apron is not part of the putting green.*

After making the stroke, though, you should repair the damage as part of the game's Etiquette.

be told of the violation before he returned his scorecard for the round and would have a penalty of two strokes rather than disqualification.

I've always been puzzled by the seeming contradiction in the Rules prohibiting me from testing the condition of a hazard in Rule 13-4 but allowing me, on the other hand, to take a firm stance in Rule 13-3. The USGA once wrestled with this contradiction before saying: "Obviously, there is a gray area between the two clauses. The gray area is a necessary evil inasmuch as it would be unfair to prohibit a player from taking a firm stance when his ball lies in the sand. Whether a player infringes on this gray area to his own advantage is often a matter which can be controlled only by his own conscience."

Some keys to the use of Rule 13-4:

• Remember that when your ball is in a hazard you may not move loose impediments in the hazard, and that loose impediments include stones and leaves. If you so much as brush one with your club during your backswing (which is before the stroke), you violate the Rule. Accidentally moving a loose impediment, provided it is not moved in making the backswing and does not improve the lie or the area of the intended swing, is not a violation.

• On the other hand, you are permitted to move movable obstructions—man-made objects, such as bottles, candy wrappers and cigarette butts.

RULE 14

STRIKING THE BALL

A "stroke" is the forward movement of the club made with the intention of fairly striking at and moving the ball, but if a player checks his downswing voluntarily before the clubhead reaches the ball he is deemed not to have made a stroke.

Definition

The ball shall be fairly struck at with the head of the club and must not be pushed, scraped or spooned.

14-1
Ball to Be Fairly Struck At

In making a stroke, a player shall not accept physical assistance or protection from the elements.
PENALTY FOR BREACH OF RULE 14-1 OR -2:
Match play—Loss of hole; Stroke play—Two strokes.

14-2
Assistance

Except as provided in the Rules, during a stipulated round the player shall not use any artificial device or unusual equipment:

a. For the purpose of gauging or measuring distance or conditions which might affect his play; or

b. Which might assist him in gripping the club, in making a stroke or in his play, except that plain gloves may be worn, resin, tape or gauze may be applied to the grip (pro-

14-3
Artificial Devices and Unusual Equipment

69

vided such application does not render the grip non-conforming under Rule 4-1c) and a towel or handkerchief may be wrapped around the grip.

PENALTY FOR BREACH OF RULE 14-3: *Disqualification.*

14-4
Striking the Ball More than Once

If a player's club strikes the ball more than once in the course of a stroke, the player shall count the stroke and *add a penalty stroke,* making two strokes in all.

14-5
Playing a Moving Ball

A player shall not play while his ball is moving.
  Exceptions:
    Ball falling off tee—Rule 11-3.
    Striking the ball more than once—Rule 14-4.
    Ball moving in water—Rule 14-6.
  When the ball begins to move only after the player has begun the stroke or the backward movement of his club for the stroke, he shall incur no penalty under this Rule for playing a moving ball, but he is not exempt from any penalty incurred under the following Rules:
    Ball at rest moved by player—Rule 18-2a.
    Ball at rest moving after address—Rule 18-2b.
    Ball at rest moving after loose impediment touched—Rule 18-2c.

14-6
Ball Moving in Water

When a ball is moving in water in a water hazard, the player may, without penalty, make a stroke, but he must not delay making his stroke in order to allow the wind or current to improve the position of the ball. A ball moving in water in a water hazard may be lifted if the player elects to invoke Rule 26.

PENALTY FOR BREACH OF RULE 14-5 or -6:
Match play—Loss of hole; Stroke play—Two strokes.

14-1. Ball to Be Fairly Struck At

The critical, if sometimes hard-to-determine difference between a genuine stroke and a push was dealt with in this Decision: "A player's ball is close to an out-of-bounds fence, but there is room behind the ball to insert an iron club or a putter and leave a space of half an inch between the ball and the face of the club. If the player plays a stroke with such a limited backswing, is he in breach of Rule 14-1?"

Answer: "It is possible to strike a ball fairly with a half-inch backswing. However, in most cases the player would be pushing the ball, contrary to Rule 14-1. In the absence of strong evidence to the contrary, it should be ruled that the player has pushed the ball.

"In order to strike the ball fairly, it must be swung at with the clubhead. If the ball is moved by any other method, it has been pushed, scraped or spooned.

"If a ball is fairly struck at, there is only momentary contact between the clubhead and the ball or whatever intervenes between the clubhead and the ball."

70

14-2. Assistance

As for Rule 14-2, the only physical assistance I can imagine would be to have someone hold me steady as I took a precarious stance on a steep slope. Even your caddie is not allowed to hold on to you. Protection against the elements, however, is something we could all use when a high wind causes rain to slant. Without this restriction you'd see caddies shielding their players from the elements with huge umbrellas.

14-3. Artificial Devices and Unusual Equipment

The best way to illustrate Rule 14-3 about artificial devices is to present a series of examples.

Not artificial devices. Using weighted head covers; wearing regular eyeglasses or contact lenses; dropping a handkerchief to determine wind conditions; applying gauze tape or wrapping a handkerchief around the grip to keep from slipping; using a booklet illustrating distances to holes from various landmarks; using a hand warmer, provided it is not also used to affect the temperature of golf balls.

Artificial devices. Using any of the following: field glasses which have a range-finder feature; an actual plumb line—a weight suspended from a string; a ball warmer during a round; an electronic instrument used to find balls which have transmitters embedded in their cores.

14-4. Striking the Ball More than Once

Nothing seems to teach the Rules better than a well-covered disaster. There's no other word to describe what happend to T. C. Chen, cruising along with a lead in the 1985 U.S. Open, when he "double-hit" a soft pitch shot. The stroke T. C. played was his third, but because of the penalty called for in Rule 14-4, his next was the fifth. He came out of that hole with an 8.

I have had my own problems with Rule 14-4. During the 1977 Memorial Tournament at Jack Nicklaus' Muirfield Village Golf Club, I tried to putt my ball out of heavy grass. When I struck the ball it tangled in the grass and I hit it again in a continuation of the same stroke. I immediately—and sorrowfully—called the penalty on myself.

14-5. Playing a Moving Ball

Frankly, I've never been able to figure out why it's necessary to have a Rule prohibiting play while a ball is moving, but now I think I understand it. Suppose your ball is at rest, poised delicately on a slope, and as you approach the ball it begins to roll—toward a water hazard or a boundary. It might be to your advantage to swat at it on the run—but that turns the game into a form of field hockey.

Golfers are often thrown for a loop by one provision of Rule 14-5. According to Rule 18-2b, if your ball moves once you've addressed it (taken your stance and, through the green, grounded your club), you are deemed to have caused it to move. Okay, suppose you lie 2 in the rough, and after you've addressed the ball and begun your stroke, your ball moves. You complete the stroke and hit the ball. Rule 14-5 says you are not exempted from Rule 18-2b; you therefore incur a one-stroke penalty and now lie 4.

14-6. Ball Moving in Water

The Rules do allow for play of a moving ball in water. If a ball is playable in water, it's often difficult to tell whether the ball is moving or not. Thus it seems only right that the player should be allowed a crack at it, moving or not. The most celebrated instance of playing a moving ball took place before I was born, during the 1938 U.S. Open at the Cherry Hills Country Club near Denver. Pro Ray Ainsley put his second shot into a creek on the par-4 16th hole and decided the ball was playable. Ainsley made fourteen strokes at the ball in the hazard. Sometimes the ball was moving when he made a stroke and sometimes it wasn't. In any event, he holed out in nineteen—the most strokes ever taken on one hole in our Open.

RULE 15

PLAYING A WRONG BALL

Definition

A "wrong ball" is any ball other than:
a. The ball in play,
b. A provisional ball or
c. In stroke play, a second ball played under Rule 3-3 or Rule 20-7b.
Note: *Ball in play includes a ball substituted for the ball in play when the player is proceeding under an applicable Rule which does not permit substitution.*

15-1
General

A player must hole out with the ball played from the teeing ground unless a Rule permits him to substitute another ball. If a player subtitutes another ball when proceeding under an applicable Rule which does not permit substitution, that ball is not a wrong ball; it becomes the ball in play and, if the error is not corrected as provided in Rule 20-6, *the player shall incur a penalty of loss of hole in match play or two strokes in stroke play.*

15-2
Match Play

If a player plays a stroke with a wrong ball except in a hazard, *he shall lose the hole.*

If a player plays any strokes in a hazard with a wrong ball, there is no penalty. Strokes played in a hazard with a wrong ball do not count in the player's score. If the wrong ball belongs to another player, its owner shall place a ball on the spot from which the wrong ball was first played.

If the player and opponent exchange balls during the play of a hole, the first to play the wrong ball other than from a hazard shall lose the hole; when this cannot be determined, the hole shall be played out with the balls exchanged.

15-3
Stroke Play

If a competitor plays a stroke or strokes with a wrong ball, *he shall incur a penalty of two strokes,* unless the only stroke or strokes played with such ball were played when it was lying in a hazard, in which case no penalty is incurred.

The competitor must correct his mistake by playing the correct ball. If he fails to correct his mistake before he plays a stroke from the next <u>teeing ground</u> or, in the case of the last hole of the round, fails to declare his intention to correct his mistake before leaving the <u>putting green</u>, *he shall be disqualified.*

Strokes played by a competitor with a wrong ball do not count in his score.

If the wrong ball belongs to another competitor, its owner shall place a ball on the spot from which the wrong ball was first played.

(Lie of ball to be placed or replaced altered—see Rule 20-3b.)

The first two sections of Rule 15 are straightforward and simple, but the third section, for stroke play, is just plain tricky and onerous. Let's tackle them in order:

General: You may not substitute balls during a hole unless specifically authorized to do so by the Rules. This precludes the use of what some golfers call "putting balls," the shiny and unscarred ones they would like to use after risking a battered veteran off the tee on a water hole.

Match Play: As soon as a player plays a wrong ball, except in a hazard, he loses the hole; in four-ball play the errant player is disqualified for that hole but there's no penalty for his partner, even if the wrong ball belonged to his partner.

Stroke Play: When a competitor plays a wrong ball, except in a hazard, he immediately suffers a two-stroke penalty and doesn't count any strokes played with the wrong ball. Moreover, if the mistake is not rectified, the penalty is disqualification. (Rectification means returning to play the correct ball before teeing off on the next hole or, if the mistake is made on the last hole, before he leaves the putting green.)

There is an amendment to Rule 15-1 among the 1988 changes which should prevent some disqualification penalties. This actually happened to club pro Jim Blair of Utah in the 1987 PGA Championship: his caddie substituted another ball in the act of cleaning it on a putting green. The ball substituted was a "wrong ball." The error was discovered during the next hole but by then it was too late. Under the old Rule 15-1 Blair was disqualified. Starting in 1988, a ball substituted in such a circumstance is no longer considered a "wrong ball." It becomes the ball in play and the penalty is two strokes. The penalty in match play is still loss of hole.

I've played a wrong ball only once in my professional career. During the pro tour's 1972 Team Championship (four-ball stroke play) at the Laurel Valley Golf Club in Ligonier, Pennsylvania, my partner was Bob Zender. We both pushed our drives to the right on a par-4 and managed to play each other's ball. We discovered the errors before either of us had played a third stroke. It meant two-stroke penalties for both of us and we had to go back and play correctly. I "birdied" the hole with the correct ball, but our score for the hole was a bogie 5.

Some Rule 15 Decisions to chew on:

• A player swings at a ball, misses and then discovers it wasn't his ball.

Answer: In match play the player made a stroke at a wrong ball and lost the hole; in stroke play he incurred a two-stroke penalty.

● "In stroke play, a competitor considered his ball lost in a water hazard, although there was not reasonable evidence to that effect. He dropped a ball behind the hazard under Rule 26-1b and played it. A fellow-competitor then questioned the competitor's procedure. What is the ruling?"

"The ball dropped behind the hazard was not substituted under an applicable Rule and thus it was not the ball in play but rather a wrong ball (Rule 15-3)—see Definitions of 'Ball in Play' and 'Wrong Ball.' The competitor incurred a penalty of two strokes for playing the ball dropped behind the hazard and he must abandon it and, if the original ball is not found within five minutes, proceed under Rule 27-1."

● A player discovers after the 6th hole that he's not playing the ball with which he started the round. What to do? The Committee must determine if the different ball is a wrong ball and must give the player the benefit of any doubt. For example, if the player might have put the different ball into play at the start of a hole, the Committee should rule in favor of the player—no penalty. But if the determination is that a wrong ball has been played, the outcomes in stroke and match play are:

Stroke play—The player is disqualified unless it's ruled that the error happened during the 6th hole, in which case rectification is possible under Rule 15-3.

Match play—If it's not possible to determine where the violation occurred the player should be penalized the loss of a hole he has won.

THE PUTTING GREEN

RULE 16

THE PUTTING GREEN

The "putting green" is all ground of the hole being played which is specially prepared for putting or otherwise defined as such by the Committee. A ball is on the putting green when any part of it touches the putting green.

A ball is "holed" when it is at rest within the circumference of the hole and all of it is below the level of the lip of the hole.

a. TOUCHING LINE OF PUTT

The line of putt must not be touched except:

(i) the player may move sand and loose soil on the putting green and other loose impediments by picking them up or by brushing them aside with his hand or a club without pressing anything down;

(ii) in addressng the ball, the player may place the club in front of the ball without pressing anything down;

(iii) in measuring—Rule 10-4;

(iv) in lifting the ball—Rule 16-1b;

(v) in pressing down a ball-marker;

(vi) in repairing old hole plugs or ball marks on the putting green—Rule 16-1c; and

(vii) in removing movable obstructions—Rule 24-1.

(Indicating line for putting on putting green—see Rule 8-2b.)

b. LIFTING BALL

A ball on the putting green may be lifted and, if desired, cleaned. A ball so lifted shall be replaced on the spot from which it was lifted.

c. REPAIR OF HOLE PLUGS AND BALL MARKS

The player may repair an old hole plug or damage to the putting green caused by the impact of a ball, whether or not the player's ball lies on the putting green. If the ball is moved

75

Don't Repair Spike Marks

The line of putt is sacrosanct. It is not to be improved unless the Rules specify exceptions —for example, repairing ball marks and removing loose impediments. This most assuredly means that irregularities on the line of putt, such as raised tufts of grass, may not be tamped down, as is being done here. (R. 16-1a)

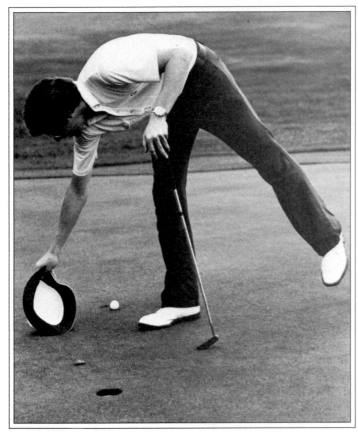

Don't Use a Hat as a Brush

You are allowed to pick up or brush aside loose impediments on the line of putt. But all you can use are your hands or a club. If anything else is used—a hat, for instance—it's a violation.

Repairing Ball Marks

Ball marks on putting greens may be repaired, even if they're on your line. As a matter of fact, they should be repaired, no matter where they are. I use a tee to loosen the soil around the mark. After the compacted soil has been loosened at several positions, I pull the turf toward the center of the damaged spot. The smoothing process can be done either with a putter, one's hand, or by stepping down on the spot. (R. 16-1c)

in the process of such repair, it shall be replaced, without penalty.

d. TESTING SURFACE

During the play of a hole, a player shall not test the surface of the putting green by rolling a ball or roughening or scraping the surface.

e. STANDING ASTRIDE OR ON LINE OF PUTT

The player shall not make a stroke on the putting green from a stance astride, or with either foot touching, the line of the putt or an extension of that line behind the ball. For the purpose of this Clause only, the line of putt does not extend beyond the hole.

f. POSITION OF CADDIE OR PARTNER

While making the stroke, the player shall not allow his caddie, his partner or his partner's caddie to position himself on or close to an extension of the line of putt behind the ball.

g. PLAYING STROKE WITH ANOTHER BALL IN MOTION

A player shall not play a stroke while another ball is in motion after a stroke on the putting green.

(Lifting ball interfering with or assisting play while another ball is in motion—see Rule 22.)

PENALTY FOR BREACH OF RULE 16-1:
Match play—Loss of hole; Stroke play—Two strokes.

16-2
Ball Overhanging Hole

When any part of the ball overhangs the lip of the hole, the player is allowed enough time to reach the hole without unreasonable delay and an additional ten seconds to determine whether the ball is at rest. If by then the ball has not fallen into the hole, it is deemed to be at rest. If the ball subsequently falls into the hole, the player is deemed to have holed out with his last stroke, and *he shall add a penalty stroke to his score* for the hole; otherwise there is no penalty under this Rule.

(Undue delay—see Rule 6-7.)

A disproportionate number of Rules incidents occur on putting greens, where all players and balls eventually converge. One of the happiest consequences of the reorganization of the Rules of Golf in 1984 was a vastly simplified presentation of the complexities of life on putting greens.

16-1a. Touching Line of Putt

The line of putt is holy ground. It is not to be touched except during the seven activities specified in 16-1a.

Here are some transgressions:

● Repairing spike or scuff marks, which would be so difficult to define for Rules purposes that a Rule permitting their repair could open the door for repair of any minor imperfections in the putting surface. It would also make the game slower, and we surely don't need that.

● Brushing aside or sopping up casual water. The same goes for dew.

- Walking or stepping on the line of putt, if the line is improved. A Decision confirms that walking on the line is okay if it's done accidentally *and* the line is not improved.
- Brushing away leaves with a hat or towel. All you can use are your hands or a club.

16-1b. Lifting Ball

The Rules used to imply that the ball had to be cleaned when it was lifted on a green. Not any more. Personally, I think the average golfer indulges in lifting and cleaning too much! We need to speed up the game.

16-1c. Repair of Hole Plugs and Ball Marks

Everyone should acquire the habit of scanning for ball marks to repair, no matter who made them.

16-1d. Testing Surface

If I could rub the surface of greens, it would help me to "read" the grain better and make putting a little easier. Putting should remain a craft that requires exquisite sensitivity.

Golfers should avoid cleaning balls by rubbing them on greens, notwithstanding a Decision that says cleaning the ball by rubbing it on the surface of the putting green does not violate the Rules, provided the act is not for the purpose of testing the surface of the green. The Decision recommends that the ball be cleaned in another manner so as to eliminate questions as to the player's intentions.

16-1e. Standing Astride or on Line of Putt

This clause bars what used to be called "straddle" putting, a variation popularized by Sam Snead. Sam's reaction was to continue to putt croquet-style, but to stand with both feet together *off* an extension of the line of putt, behind the ball.

16-1f. Position of Caddie or Partner

There was a time when prominent players, Johnny Miller foremost among them, had their caddies crouch behind them to give counsel on alignment. It was stopped by the Rulesmakers, who argued that the practice was making the caddie into something more than he should be.

Partners in four-ball events should be aware of this clause, since it applies to them as well.

Incidentally, LPGA star Betsy King often has her caddie positioned behind her to check Betsy's alignment on shots played from fairways. That's not a violation since Rule 16-1f applies only on putting greens.

16-1g. Playing Stroke with Another Ball in Motion

That's easy. No one plays or touches his ball while another ball is in motion.

16-2. Ball Overhanging Hole

The player is allowed enough time to reach the hole without unreasonable delay, plus ten seconds.

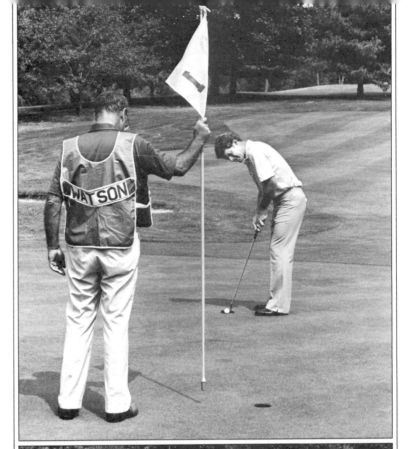

Direction for Putting

My caddie or my partner can use the flagstick to point to the line of putt. But if he touches the putting green in front of, to the side of, or behind the hole, I'm penalized. (R. 8-2)

The Rule has been amended in 1988 because of the controversial Denis Watson incident during the 1985 Open. Denis waited more than thirty seconds for a ball to fall, which it did. He was penalized two strokes and was eventually runner-up to Andy North by one shot.

The Rule has been modified to provide that, if a ball overhanging the hole falls in after the time limit of ten seconds has expired, the player is deemed to have holed out with his last stroke and he incurs a penalty stroke. If the ball does not fall into the hole, there is no penalty—assuming the player does not unduly delay play. Thus, the score is going to be the same whether the ball falls in or not and Denis Watson's 5 of 1985 becomes a 4 in 1988.

These are a couple of obvious ramifications in match play:

• If a player's ball is overhanging the hole, he's entitled to his ten seconds. Should an opponent concede the next stroke before ten seconds by knocking the ball away, the opponent has infringed the player's right and loses the hole.

• After ten seconds, the player may no longer insist the ball is moving. In match play, his opponent may then concede the putt.

RULE 17

THE FLAGSTICK

17-1
Flagstick Attended, Removed or Held Up

Before and during the stroke, the player may have the flagstick attended, removed or held up to indicate the position of the hole. This may be done only on the authority of the player before he plays his stroke.

If the flagstick is attended, removed or held up by an opponent, a fellow-competitor or the caddie of either with the player's knowledge and no objection is made, the player shall be deemed to have authorized it. If a player or a caddie attends, removes or holds up the flagstick or stands near the hole while a stroke is being played, he shall be deemed to be attending the flagstick until the ball comes to rest.

If the flagstick is not attended before the stroke is played, it shall not be attended or removed while the ball is in motion.

17-2
Unauthorized Attendance

a. MATCH PLAY
In match play, an opponent or his caddie shall not attend, remove or hold up the flagstick without the player's knowledge or authority while the player is making a stroke or his ball is in motion.

b. STROKE PLAY
In stroke play, if a fellow-competitor or his caddie attends, removes or holds up the flagstick without the competitor's knowledge or authority while the competitor is making a stroke or his ball is in motion, *the fellow-competitor shall incur the penalty* for breach of this Rule. In such circumstances, if the competitor's ball strikes the flagstick or the person attending it, the competitor incurs no penalty and the

81

Flagstick Held Aloft

When a green is elevated, it isn't always possible to see the flagstick when you address the ball. In that case, the flagstick may be held up at the hole (1), and it can be attended in that manner during the stroke. But if the flagstick is held aloft away from the hole (2), the caddie has to get off the line before the stroke is played.

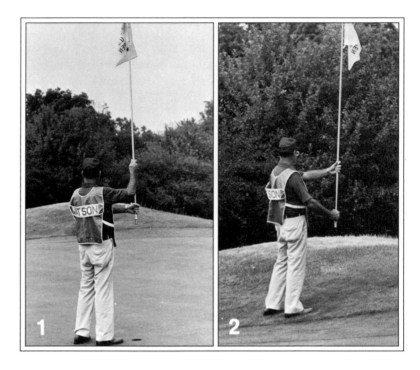

ball shall be played as it lies, except that, if the stroke was played from the putting green, the stroke shall be replayed.

PENALTY FOR BREACH OF RULE 17-1 or -2:
Match play—Loss of hole; Stroke play—Two strokes.

17-3
Ball Striking Flagstick or Attendant

The player's ball shall not strike:

a. The flagstick when attended, removed or held up by the player, his partner or either of their caddies, or by another person with the player's knowledge or authority; or

b. The player's caddie, his partner or his partner's caddie when attending the flagstick, or another person attending the flagstick with the player's knowledge or authority, or <u>equipment</u> carried by any such person; or

c. The flagstick in the hole, unattended, when the ball has been played from the <u>putting green.</u>

PENALTY FOR BREACH OF RULE 17-3:
Match play—Loss of hole; Stroke play—Two strokes, and the ball shall be played as it lies.

17-4
Ball Resting Against Flagstick

If the ball rests against the flagstick when it is in the hole, the player or another person authorized by him may move or remove the flagstick and if the ball falls into the hole, the player shall be deemed to have holed out at his last stroke; otherwise, the ball, if <u>moved</u>, shall be placed on the lip of the hole, without penalty.

The flagstick exists in order to indicate the location of the hole. Its incidental use as a backstop has been a subject of controversy and

82

the cause of many Rules changes over the years. Now, happily, the Rule has settled into a form we can all understand:

• If your ball is *on* the putting green and it strikes the flagstick, whether it's attended or unattended, the penalty is loss of hole in match play or two strokes in stroke play.

• If your ball is *off* the green, you may use the flagstick as a backstop. There is no penalty for striking it as long as it is not attended.

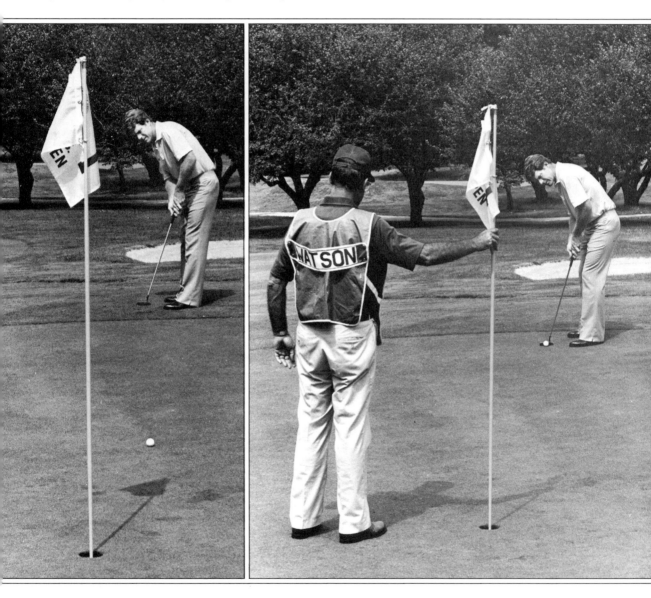

Striking the Flagstick
When I putt from off the green, I may prefer to have the flagstick remain in the hole, *since there's no penalty for striking the flagstick from off the green. But when the ball is played from on the green,* *there is a penalty for striking the flagstick, which should either be attended or set aside. (R. 17-3)*

83

BALL MOVED, DEFLECTED OR STOPPED

BALL AT REST MOVED

Definitions

A ball is deemed to have "moved" if it leaves its position and comes to rest in any other place.

An "outside agency" is any agency not part of the match or, in stroke play, not part of a competitor's side, and includes a referee, a marker, an observer or a forecaddie. Neither wind nor water is an outside agency.

"Equipment" is anything used, worn or carried by or for the player except any ball he has played at the hole being played and any small object, such as a coin or a tee, when used to mark the position of a ball or the extent of an area in which a ball is to be dropped. Equipment includes a golf cart, whether or not motorized. If such a cart is shared by more than one player, its status under the Rules is the same as that of a caddie employed by more than one player. See "Caddie."

A player has "addressed the ball" when he has taken his stance and has also grounded his club, except that in a hazard a player has addressed the ball when he has taken his stance.

Taking the "stance" consists in a player placing his feet in position for and preparatory to making a stroke.

18-1

By Outside Agency

If a ball at rest is moved by an outside agency, the player shall incur no penalty and the ball shall be replaced before the player plays another stroke.

(Player's ball at rest moved by another ball—see Rule 18-5.)

a. GENERAL

When a player's ball is in play, if:

(i) the player, his partner or either of their caddies lifts or moves it, touches it purposely (except with a club in the act of addressing it) or causes it to move except as permitted by a Rule, or

18-2

By Player, Partner, Caddie or Equipment

Stop that Outside Agency!

The player is Johnny Bulla; the scene the 1950 U.S. Open Championship at the Merion Golf Club. An outside agency snatched Bulla's ball and made a clean getaway. Whenever an outside agency —be it human, animal or mechanical—moves a ball, the ball is to be replaced without penalty. If the outside agency is a successful thief, another ball may be substituted. (R. 18-1)

85

(ii) equipment of the player or his partner causes the ball to move,

the player shall incur a penalty stroke. The ball shall be replaced unless the movement of the ball occurs after the player has begun his swing and he does not discontinue his swing.

Under the Rules no penalty is incurred if a player accidentally causes his ball to move in the following circumstances:

In measuring to determine which ball farther from hole—Rule 10-4

In searching for covered ball in hazard or for ball in casual water, ground under repair, etc.—Rule 12-1

In the process of repairing hole plug or ball mark—Rule 16-1c

In the process of removing loose impediment on putting green—Rule 18-2c

In the process of lifting ball under a Rule—Rule 20-1

In the process of placing or replacing ball under a Rule—Rule 20-3a

In complying with Rule 22 relating to lifting ball interfering with or assisting play

In removal of movable obstruction—Rule 24-1.

b. BALL MOVING AFTER ADDRESS

If a player's ball in play moves after he has addressed it (other than as a result of a stroke), the player shall be deemed to have moved the ball and *shall incur a penalty stroke.* The player shall replace the ball unless the movement of the ball occurs after he has begun his swing and he does not discontinue his swing.

c. BALL MOVING AFTER LOOSE IMPEDIMENT TOUCHED

Through the green, if the ball moves after any loose impediment lying within a club-length of it has been touched by the player, his partner or either of their caddies and before the player has addressed it, the player shall be deemed to have moved the ball and *shall incur a penalty stroke.* The player shall replace the ball unless the movement of the ball occurs after he has begun his swing and he does not discontinue his swing.

On the putting green, if the ball moves in the process of removing any loose impediment, it shall be replaced without penalty.

18-3
By Opponent, Caddie or Equipment in Match Play

a. DURING SEARCH

If, during search for a player's ball, it is moved by an opponent, his caddie or his equipment, no penalty is incurred and the player shall replace the ball.

b. OTHER THAN DURING SEARCH

If, other than during search for a ball, the ball is touched or moved by an opponent, his caddie or his equipment, except as otherwise provided in the Rules, *the opponent shall incur a penalty stroke.* The player shall replace the ball.

(Ball moved in measuring to determine which ball farther from the hole—see Rule 10-4.)

(Playing a wrong ball—see Rule 15-2.)

(Ball moved in complying with Rule 22 relating to lifting ball interfering with or assisting play.)

If a competitor's ball is moved by a fellow-competitor, his caddie or his <u>equipment</u>, no penalty is incurred. The competitor shall replace his ball.

(Playing a wrong ball—see Rule 15-3.)

If a ball in play and at rest is moved by another ball in motion after a stroke, the moved ball shall be replaced.

PENALTY FOR BREACH OF RULE:

Match play—Loss of hole; Stroke play—Two strokes.

*If a player who is required to replace a ball fails to do so, he shall incur the general penalty for breach of Rule 18 but no additional penalty under Rule 18 shall be applied.

Note 1: *If a ball to be replaced under this Rule is not immediately recoverable, another ball may be substituted.*

Note 2: *If it is impossible to determine the spot on which a ball is to be placed, see Rule 20-3c.*

18-4
By Fellow-Competitor, Caddie or Equipment in Stroke Play

18-5
By Another Ball

The 1988 Rules contain a welcome simplification in Rule 18, which deals with a ball at rest moved in various circumstances. Now, in *every* case, the ball must be replaced. (Before 1988 when a ball moved after it was addressed, the procedure required that the ball be played from its new position.)

Rule 18 takes us through the tangle of possibilities that occur when a ball at rest is moved. Let's consider each part of Rule 18:

18-1. By Outside Agency

When your ball is moved by a dog or by a golfer playing on another hole, it's been moved by an outside agency and you *must* replace the ball. As is often the case, you may not know the spot where the ball lay when it was moved. In that case, according to Rule 20-3c, you drop as near as possible to where the ball lay, not nearer the hole, of course, but with one exception: If the ball was moved from a putting green it is to be placed, not dropped, whether or not the spot is known. No penalty. If you can't find your ball and think, but don't know for sure, that it may have been moved by an outside agency, all the available testimony and facts must be considered. To proceed under Rule 18-1, there must be "reasonable evidence" to that effect. In the absence of such evidence, the ball must be treated as a lost ball, which means stroke and distance.

18-2. By Player, Partner, Caddie or Equipment

Caution: If you so much as reach down and touch your ball except as the Rules allow, there is a penalty stroke. The onus is on you to know that the Rules give you special license whenever you lift your ball. Notice that this Rule lists every instance (eight in all) when a player may move his ball accidentally and not be penalized. It's worth your while to know them.

Don't overlook the word "equipment." A Definition reveals that a golf cart is part of a player's equipment. When a player runs over his ball while driving a cart, he has violated this Rule.

The key word in Clause b is "deemed." Once you've addressed the ball and it moves, that's it—a penalty. When it's windy or when the ball is perched in some precarious position, I take the precaution of not grounding my club and have therefore not addressed it. Remember —a Definition of "addressing the ball" tells us that grounding a club is part of addressing a ball through the green.

That word "deemed" pops up again in Clause c. If you move a twig next to your ball and the ball then moves, you can argue yourself blue in the face in claiming that the movement of the twig didn't cause the ball to move. You are "deemed" to have caused the ball to move.

18-3. By Opponent, Caddie or Equipment in Match Play

If your opponent accidentally moves your ball while he's being good enough to help you look for it, he is not penalized. Fair enough. But if your opponent accidentally moves your ball in any other situation he incurs a penalty of one stroke. You must replace your ball in any case. If not, you lose the hole.

18-4. By Fellow-Competitor, Caddie or Equipment in Stroke Play

Now we're talking about stroke play, and the proper terminology calls for the use of "fellow-competitor," who is neither your "opponent" nor your "partner." He's someone you're paired with in stroke play; he becomes an outside agency in stroke play; and he's not penalized for moving your ball. Whenever your ball at rest is moved you must replace it.

18-5. By Another Ball

Some golfers cling to the pre-1984 Rule giving an option to a player whose ball was moved by an opponent's ball in match play. There is no option. The ball is to be replaced.

RULE 19

BALL IN MOTION DEFLECTED OR STOPPED

Definitions

An "outside agency" is any agency not part of the match or, in stroke play, not part of a competitor's side, and includes a referee, a marker, an observer or a forecaddie. Neither wind nor water is an outside agency.

"Equipment' is anything used, worn or carried by or for the player except any ball he has played at the hole being played and any small object, such as a coin or a tee, when used to mark the position of a ball or the extent of an area in which a ball is to be dropped. Equipment includes a golf cart, whether or not motorized. If such a cart is shared by more than one player, its status under the Rules is the same as that of a caddie employed by more than one player. See "Caddie."

If a ball in motion is accidentally deflected or stopped by any outside agency, it is a rub of the green, no penalty is incurred and the ball shall be played as it lies except:

a. If a ball in motion after a stroke other than on the putting green comes to rest in or on any moving or animate outside agency, the player shall, through the green or in a hazard, drop the ball, or on the putting green place the ball, as near as possible to the spot where the outside agency was when the ball came to rest in or on it, and

b. If a ball in motion after a stroke on the putting green is deflected or stopped by, or comes to rest in or on, any living or animate outside agency except a worm or an insect, the stroke shall be canceled and the ball shall be replaced.

If the ball is not immediately recoverable, another ball may be substituted.

(Player's ball deflected or stopped by another ball—see Rule 19-5.)

Note: *If the referee or the Committee determines that a competitor's ball has been purposely deflected or stopped by an* outside agency, *Rule 1-4 applies to the competitor. If the outside agency is a fellow-competitor or his caddie, Rule 1-2 applies to the fellow-competitor.*

19-1

By Outside Agency

a. MATCH PLAY

If a player's ball is accidentally deflected or stopped by himself, his partner or either of their caddies or equipment, *he shall lose the hole.*

b. STROKE PLAY

If a competitor's ball is accidentally deflected or stopped by himself, his partner or either of their caddies or equipment, *the competitor shall incur a penalty of two strokes.* The ball shall be played as it lies, except when it comes to rest in or on the competitor's, his partner's or either of their caddies' clothes or equipment, in which case the competitor shall through the green or in a hazard drop the ball, or on the putting green place the ball, as near as possible to where the article was when the ball came to rest in or on it.

Exception: Dropped ball—see Rule 20-2a.

(Ball purposely deflected or stopped by player, partner or caddie—see Rule 1-2.)

19-2

By Player, Partner, Caddie or Equipment

If a player's ball is accidentally deflected or stopped by an opponent, his caddie or his equipment, no penalty is incurred. The player may play the ball as it lies or, before another stroke is played by either side, cancel the stroke and replay it (see Rule 20-5). If the player elects to replay the

19-3

By Opponent, Caddie or Equipment in Match Play

89

stroke and the original ball is not immediately recoverable, another ball may be substituted.

If the ball has come to rest in or on the opponent's or his caddie's clothes or equipment, the player may <u>through the green</u> or in a <u>hazard</u> drop the ball, or on the <u>putting green</u> place the ball, as near as possible to where the article was when the ball came to rest in or on it.

Exception: Ball striking person attending flagstick—see Rule 17-3b.

(Ball purposely deflected or stopped by opponent or caddie —see Rule 1-2.)

19-4
By Fellow-Competitor, Caddie or Equipment in Stroke Play

See Rule 19-1 regarding ball deflected by outside agency.

19-5
By a Ball at Rest

If a player's ball in motion after a stroke is deflected or stopped by a ball at rest, the player shall play his ball as it lies. In stroke play, if both balls lay on the <u>putting green</u> prior to the stroke, *the player incurs a penalty of two strokes.* Otherwise, no penalty is incurred.

If a player's ball in motion after a stroke is deflected or stopped by another ball in motion, the player shall play his ball as it lies. There is no penalty unless the player was in breach of Rule 16-1g, in which case *he shall incur the penalty for breach of that Rule.*

Exception: Ball in motion after a stroke on the putting green deflected or stopped by moving or animate outside agency—see Rule 19-1b.

PENALTY FOR BREACH OF RULE:
Match play—Loss of hole; Stroke play—Two strokes.

Rule 18 just took us through the tangle of how to proceed when a ball *at rest* is moved. Rule 19 moves on to the problems that occur when a ball *in motion* is accidentally deflected or stopped. Rule 1-2 deals with purposeful deflection.

19-1. By Outside Agency

The phrase "rub of the green" has drifted out of golf into everyday English, where it's generally taken to mean a bit of bad luck. Actually, it can work either way. If a ball bounces out of bounds after striking a cart path, that's one "rub of the green"; but if your ball is headed toward out of bounds and it's deflected by a tree onto the putting green, that too is a "rub of the green."

19-2. By Player, Partner, Caddie or Equipment

The standard match play penalty of loss of hole applies when a player's ball is deflected by himself, his partner, their caddies or their equipment (including a golf cart). In four-ball match play, only the player whose ball is involved is out of the hole.

In stroke play, it's a two-stroke penalty situation.

19-3. By Opponent, Caddie or Equipment in Match Play

Assuming the deflection by an opponent, the opponent's caddie or equipment is accidental, there is no penalty and the owner of the ball has an unusual choice. He can either play the ball as it lies or opt to cancel the stroke and play the stroke over.

19-4. By Fellow-Competitor, Caddie or Equipment in Stroke Play

It's just the same as in 19-1. There's no penalty *unless* the deflection is deliberate, in which case the offending party is in big trouble. A Committee, in equity, may disqualify a fellow-competitor who purposely stops another ball.

19-5. By a Ball at Rest

There's no penalty when a moving ball is deflected or stopped by a ball at rest, with one glaring exception: in stroke play only, when both balls are on the putting green before the stroke is played, the player whose ball is deflected suffers a two-stroke penalty. He plays his ball where it then lies; the other player must replace.

A 1988 amendment to Rule 19-5 says that when two balls in motion collide there is no penalty and the balls shall then be played as they lie.

A couple of Rule 19 Decisions:

● A ball struck a piece of maintenance equipment and was deflected out of bounds. The player claimed she should not be penalized on the ground that the equipment wasn't supposed to be there.

Answer: The ball must be treated as out of bounds. A rather harsh rub of the green, but there you have it.

● A player, in stroke play, hits a ball off line; the ball first hits his bag and then his caddie. Is the player penalized four strokes for two violations of Rule 19-2?

Answer: No. Generally, a single penalty is applied to several instances of a breach of a Rule in connection with a single stroke. For example, soling the club by touching the ground or water with it time and again in a hazard entails a single penalty. Ah, but in this case, if the ball had struck his caddie and then gone out of bounds, he would be subject to the two-stroke and stroke-and-distance penalties.

RELIEF SITUATIONS AND PROCEDURE

RULE 20

LIFTING, DROPPING AND PLACING; PLAYING FROM WRONG PLACE

20-1
Lifting

A ball to be lifted under the Rules may be lifted by the player, his partner or another person authorized by the player. In any such case, the player shall be responsible for any breach of the Rules.

The position of the ball shall be marked before it is lifted under a Rule which requires it to be replaced. If it is not marked, the player *shall incur a penalty of one stroke* and the ball shall be replaced. If it is not replaced, *the player shall incur the general penalty* for breach of this Rule but no additional penalty under Rule 20-1 shall be applied.

If a ball or a ball-marker is accidentally moved in the process of lifting the ball under a Rule or marking its position, no penalty is incurred and the ball or the ball-marker shall be replaced.

Note: *The position of a ball to be lifted should be marked by placing a ball-marker, a small coin or other similar object immediately behind the ball. If the ball-marker interferes with the play,* stance *or* stroke *of another player, it should be placed one or more clubhead-lengths to one side.*

20-2
Dropping and Re-dropping

a. BY WHOM AND HOW

A ball to be dropped under the Rules shall be dropped by the player himself. He shall stand erect, hold the ball at shoulder height and arm's length and drop it. If a ball is dropped by any other person or in any other manner and the error is not corrected as provided in Rule 20-6, *the player shall incur a penalty stroke.*

If the ball touches the player, his partner, either of their caddies or their equipment before or after it strikes the ground, the ball shall be re-dropped, without penalty. There is no limit to the number of times a ball shall be re-dropped in such circumstances.

(Taking action to influence position or movement of ball—see Rule 1-2.)

b. WHERE TO DROP

When a ball is to be dropped, it shall be dropped as near as possible to the spot where the ball lay, but not nearer the hole, except when a Rule permits or requires it to be dropped elsewhere. If a ball is to be dropped in a <u>hazard</u>, the ball shall be dropped in and come to rest in that hazard.

How to Drop
Here's the new dropping procedure, introduced in 1984. Simply extend your arm horizontally and drop the ball. That's all there is to it.

You can do it off to one side (left) or directly in front of you (right). But do remember not to use the pre-1984 procedure of dropping over your shoulder.

Geometry of Ball Dropping

Here's a common drop situation. The ball lies in ground under repair at X. First the player determines the nearest point of relief, which in this illustration is at Y— just outside the ground under repair area. The player must drop within one club-length of Y, but he can't drop in the shaded area because all of that area is either closer to the hole or within ground under repair. That leaves him with the white area. The ball remains in play if it's dropped at Point A even though it rolls outside the circle to Point B— which is less than two club-lengths from A.
(R. 25-1b)

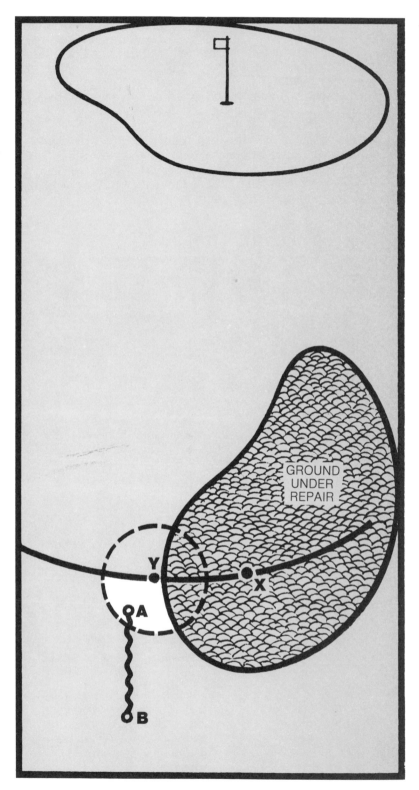

Note: *A ball when dropped must first strike the ground where the applicable Rule requires it to be dropped. If it is not so dropped, Rules 20-6 and -7 apply.*

c. WHEN TO RE-DROP

A dropped ball shall be re-dropped without penalty if it:

(i) rolls into a hazard;

(ii) rolls out of a hazard;

(iii) rolls onto a putting green;

(iv) rolls out of bounds;

(v) rolls back into the condition from which relief was taken under Rule 24-2 (immovable obstruction) or Rule 25 (abnormal ground conditions and wrong putting green);

(vi) rolls and comes to rest more than two club-lengths from where it first struck the ground; or

(vii) rolls and comes to rest nearer the hole than its original position unless otherwise permitted by the Rules.

If the ball again rolls into such position, it shall be placed as near as possible to the spot where it first struck the ground when re-dropped.

If a ball to be re-dropped or placed under this Rule is not immediately recoverable, another ball may be substituted.

20-3

Placing and Replacing

a. BY WHOM AND WHERE

A ball to be placed under the Rules shall be placed by the player or his partner. A ball to be replaced shall be replaced by the player, his partner or the person who lifted or moved it. In any such case, the player shall be responsible for any breach of the Rules.

If a ball or a ball-marker is accidentally moved in the process of placing or replacing the ball, no penalty is incurred and the ball or the ball-marker shall be replaced.

b. LIE OF BALL TO BE PLACED OR REPLACED ALTERED

If the original lie of a ball to be placed or replaced has been altered:

(i) except in a hazard, the ball shall be placed in the nearest lie most similar to the original lie which is not more than one club-length from the original lie, not nearer the hole and not in a hazard;

(ii) in a water hazard, the ball shall be placed in accordance with Clause (i) above, except that the ball must be placed in the water hazard;

(iii) in a bunker, the original lie shall be recreated as nearly as possible and the ball shall be placed in that lie.

c. SPOT NOT DETERMINABLE

If it is impossible to determine the spot where the ball is to be placed:

(i) through the green, the ball shall be dropped as near as possible to the place where it lay but not nearer the hole or in a hazard;

(ii) in a hazard, the ball shall be dropped in the hazard as near as possible to the place where it lay but not nearer the hole;

(iii) on the <u>putting green</u>, the ball shall be placed as near as possible to the place where it lay but not nearer the hole or in a hazard.

d. BALL FAILS TO REMAIN ON SPOT

If a ball when placed fails to remain on the spot on which it was placed, it shall be replaced without penalty. If it still fails to remain on that spot:

(i) except in a <u>hazard</u>, it shall be placed at the nearest spot not nearer the hole or in a hazard where it can be placed at rest;

(ii) in a hazard, it shall be placed in the hazard at the nearest spot not nearer the hole where it can be placed at rest.

PENALTY FOR BREACH OF RULE 20-1, -2 OR -3:
Match play—Loss of hole; Stroke play—Two strokes.

20-4
When Ball Dropped or Placed Is in Play

If the player's <u>ball in play</u> has been lifted, it is again in play when dropped or placed.

A substituted ball becomes the ball in play if it is dropped or placed under an applicable Rule, whether or not such Rule permits substitution. A ball substituted under an inapplicable Rule is a <u>wrong ball</u>.

20-5
Playing Next Stroke from Where Previous Stroke Played

When, under the Rules, a player elects or is required to play his next <u>stroke</u> from where a previous stroke was played, he shall proceed as follows: If the stroke is to be played from the <u>teeing ground</u>, the ball to be played shall be played from anywhere within the teeing ground and may be teed; if the stroke is to be played from <u>through the green</u> or a <u>hazard</u>, it shall be dropped; if the stroke is to be played on the <u>putting green</u>, it shall be placed.

PENALTY FOR BREACH OF RULE 20-5:
Match play—Loss of hole; Stroke play—Two strokes.

20-6
Lifting Ball Wrongly Dropped or Placed

A ball dropped or placed in a wrong place or otherwise not in accordance with the Rules but not played may be lifted, without penalty, and the player shall then proceed correctly.

20-7
Playing from Wrong Place

For a ball played outside teeing ground, see Rule 11-4.

a. MATCH PLAY

If a player plays a stroke with a ball which has been dropped or placed in a wrong place, *he shall lose the hole.*

b. STROKE PLAY

If a competitor plays a stroke with (i) his original ball which has been dropped or placed in a wrong place, (ii) a substituted ball which has been dropped or placed under an applicable Rule but in a wrong place or (iii) his ball in play when it has been moved and not replaced in a case where the Rules require replacement, *he shall,* provided a serious breach has not occurred, *incur the penalty prescribed by the applicable Rule* and play out the hole with the ball.

If, after playing from a wrong place, a competitor becomes

aware of that fact and believes that a serious breach may be involved, he may, provided he has not played a stroke from the next teeing ground or, in the case of the last hole of the round, left the putting green, declare that he will play out the hole with a second ball dropped or placed in accordance with the Rules. The competitor shall report the facts to the Committee before returning his score card; if he fails to do so, *he shall be disqualified.* The Committee shall determine whether a serious breach of the Rule occurred. If so, the score with the second ball shall count and *the competitor shall add two penalty strokes to his score with that ball.*

If a serious breach has occurred and the competitor has failed to correct it as prescribed above, *he shall be disqualified.*

Note: *If a competitor plays a second ball, penalty strokes incurred by playing the ball ruled not to count and strokes subsequenty taken with that ball shall be disregarded.*

20-1. Lifting

Rule 20, to be used properly, requires a good deal of prior knowledge. First, the ball should not be lifted unless the golfer is certain that the Rules authorize him to pick it up. Second, having lifted the ball, he should know whether the ball should be dropped or placed when it is put back into play. (If it is to be replaced, he must mark its position.) If the ball is to be dropped, he should know where he may drop it. In some cases the ball must be dropped as near as possible to the spot from which it was lifted, such as when the ball is embedded in a fairway; in others there's a one-club-length tolerance from the nearest point of relief, as when taking relief from ground under repair; and in others there's a two-club-length leeway—*e.g.,* dropping on either side of a lateral water hazard. Here's a key: when the extent of relief is one club-length, there is no penalty; when the extent is two club-lengths, a penalty is involved.

20-2. Dropping and Re-dropping

The dropping method is simple. The player only has to stand erect, hold the ball at shoulder height and arm's length—and drop it. It doesn't matter what he's facing or where he's looking.

If you drop the ball in any other manner, including the old "over the shoulder" way, you will incur a penalty stroke—unless you remember, or are reminded, to pick it up and drop correctly, a corrective action permitted by Clause 6 of this Rule.

It often happens that when a player drops a ball, the slope of the ground is such that the ball rolls more than two club-lengths or nearer the hole. Rule 20-2c calls for a three-step procedure:

1. Ball is dropped and it rolls nearer the hole or more than two club-lengths.

2. Ball is dropped again and it again rolls nearer the hole or more than two club-lengths.

3. Ball is then *placed* on the spot where it first touched the ground when it was dropped the second time.

Rule 20-2c pulls together all the mandatory "re-drops."

Marking a Ball

When a ball anywhere on the course is to be lifted, its position must be marked if the ball is to be replaced. I use a coin (1) and place it immediately behind the ball (2) before lifting the ball (3). When the coin interferes with another player it's moved the length of one or more putterheads. To make sure I can replace the coin exactly where it was, I first select a reference point—often a tree (4)—before setting down my putter between the coin and the reference point (5). The last step is to move the coin. Remember that the ball must be returned to its original position. (R. 20-1)

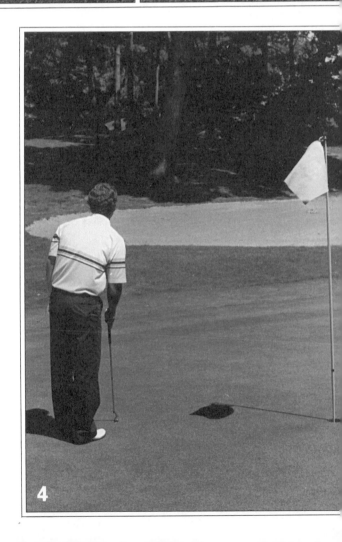

20-3. Placing and Replacing

Placing isn't as complicated as dropping but it can lead to problems. Rule 20-3b deals with what to do when the lie of a ball to be placed has been "altered." Imagine that your ball and your opponent's touch each other in a fairway. He's away, so you mark and lift your ball. When he plays, he takes a divot and effectively demolishes your lie. You don't have to place the ball in the hole, nor do you replace the divot and put your ball on it. What you do is place your ball as near as possible to its original position in "the nearest lie most similar to the original lie which is not more than one club-length from the original lie, not nearer the hole and not in a hazard."

In a bunker, however, the procedure is dramatically different. When a lie is "altered"—which happens inevitably when balls come to rest adjacent to each other—the original lie is to be *re-created* as nearly as possible. This means that the player gets to smooth the sand and place his ball atop it, if that's the way it was originally; conversely, it means he has to plug his ball into the sand if that was its original lie.

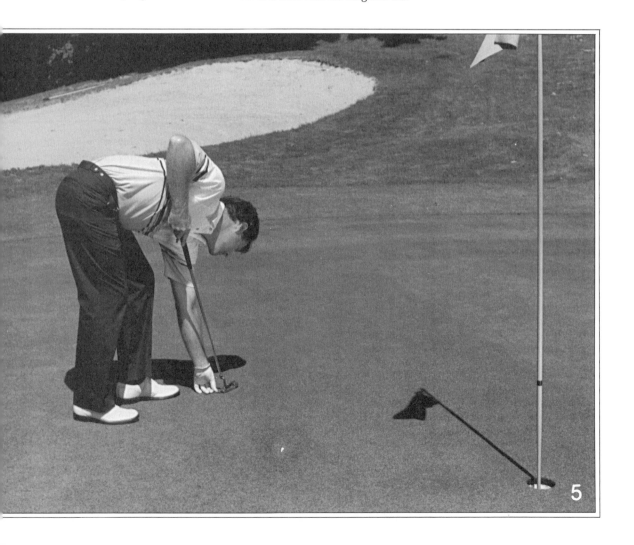

5

20-4. When Ball Dropped or Placed Is in Play

Jack Nicklaus is superb when it comes to understanding and applying the Rules, but he once cost himself dearly by failing to understand Rule 20-4. Worse yet, it happened in the Masters on the 15th hole. His ball had come to rest against a spectator's stool, and the ball moved when the stool was moved. Jack then correctly replaced his ball on a bank that sloped sharply toward the green. (See Rule 24-1.) There was very little grass to support the ball and Jack was faced with a delicate little pitch. It was not likely he'd get down in two. Ben Crenshaw, with whom Jack was paired, was away, and as Ben prepared to play and then did play, Jack surveyed the green. When he looked back, he saw that his ball had rolled down the slope about fifteen yards to the edge of the green. The ball had actually been at rest for about one minute. Jack's instinctive sportsmanship suggested to him that he had to put the ball back up on the slope. He conferred with an official, and they agreed that the ball had to be replaced. They were wrong! Once the ball was properly placed and remained at rest for a few seconds, it was in play. When it subsequently moved, it was in play at the new position and should have been played from there. As it happened, Jack took three to get down from the slope and made a par 5. Had he played from the edge of the green, he would have been putting for an eagle 3 and almost surely would have made a birdie 4. Moreover, Jack's sportsmanship could have caused him two penalty strokes, under Rule 18, for picking up his ball when he was not entitled to, and for failing to replace it on the spot from which it was lifted. There was no penalty, since a player is entitled to assume that an official's ruling is correct.

Rule 20-6. Lifting Ball Wrongly Dropped or Placed

Rule 20-6 gets the player off the hook if he errs in dropping or placing, provided he hasn't made the next stroke. Thus if a player taking relief from a cart path—an obstruction—drops more than one club-length away from the nearest point of relief and immediately learns of the error, he can correct the mistake without penalty.

Rule 20-7. Playing from Wrong Place

The wording of Rule 20-7 is a little on the heavy side. An example of a "wrong place" incident is when a ball is dropped more than one club-length from the nearest point of relief from interference by a cart path.

When that happens in match play, the penalty is loss of hole as soon as the offender plays a stroke.

But in stroke play the penalty is two strokes, because that's what is called for by the Rule governing obtructions. If, after making the next stroke, the "wrong place" violation is made known to the player, he must play on and hole out. He can't rectify the mistake once the stroke is made, unless a "serious breach" is involved.

A "serious breach" is one that would give a player an inordinate advantage. Imagine a water hazard thirty yards in diameter right up against the green. The ball enters the hazard in such a way that the player, in taking relief, must drop behind the hazard. But let's assume the player instead drops on the far side of the hazard, next to the green. He hasn't negotiated the hazard. That's a serious breach, and unless it's rectified as permitted in Rule 20-7, the penalty in stroke play is disqualification.

RULE 21

CLEANING BALL

A ball on the putting green may be cleaned when lifted under Rule 16-1b. Elsewhere, a ball may be cleaned when lifted except when it has been lifted:

a. To determine if it is unfit for play (Rule 5-3);

b. For identification (Rule 12-2), in which case it may be cleaned only to the extent necessary for identification; or

c. Because it is interfering with or assisting play (Rule 22).

If a player cleans his ball during play of a hole except as provided in this Rule, *he shall incur a penalty of one stroke* and the ball, if lifted, shall be replaced.

If a player who is required to replace a ball fails to do so, *he shall incur the penalty* for breach of Rule 20-3a, but no additional penalty under Rule 21 shall be applied.

Exception: If a player incurs a penalty for failing to act in accordance with Rule 5-3, 12-2 or 22, no additional penalty under Rule 21 shall be applied.

Rule 21, happily, has been turned on it head with the 1988 revisions. Instead of listing all the situations which allow for cleaning a ball after it's lifted, Rule 21 now says the ball can be cleaned every time it's lifted with three exceptions—(1) when it's been lifted to determine if it's not fit for play; (2) for identification; (3) because it is interfering with or assisting play. The Rules provide a specific exemption in the third instance and that happens when the lifted ball is on a putting green. See Rule 16-1b.

RULE 22

BALL INTERFERING WITH OR ASSISTING PLAY

Any player may:

a. Lift his ball if he considers that it might assist any other player or

b. Have any other ball lifted if he considers that it might interfere with his play or assist the play of any other player, but this may not be done while another ball is in motion. In stroke play, a player required to lift his ball may play first rather than lift. A ball lifted under this Rule shall be replaced.

If a ball is accidentally moved in complying with this Rule, no penalty is incurred and the ball shall be replaced.

PENALTY FOR BREACH OF RULE:
Match play—Loss of hole; Stroke play—Two strokes.

Rule 22 covers all the situations in which a ball interferes with or assists play.

An opponent or fellow-competitor is always permitted to lift his ball if he considers that it might assist any other player.

Before 1984, the Rules provided that in singles match play the player who is away "controlled" the opponent's ball in the sense of having the right to require him to leave it or lift it. No longer can the ball adjacent to or beyond a hole be used as a kind of backstop. The owner of the potential backstop can protect himself by lifting his ball. But if he doesn't and the ball is moved by the putted ball of an opponent, the moved ball *must* be replaced. The owner of the moved ball does not have the option of playing it from its new place.

In four-ball play, be it match or stroke, that same principle applies. Any player can have any ball lifted if he thinks it might interfere with his play or, because of its location, help the play of an opponent.

RULE 23

LOOSE IMPEDIMENTS

Definition

"Loose impediments" are natural objects such as stones, leaves, twigs, branches and the like, dung, worms and insects and casts or heaps made by them, provided they are not fixed or growing, are not solidly embedded and do not adhere to the ball.

Sand and loose soil are loose impediments on the <u>putting green</u> but not elsewhere.

Snow and ice are either <u>casual water</u> or loose impediments, at the option of the player, except that manufactured ice is an <u>obstruction</u>.

Dew is not a loose impediment.

Relief

Except when both the <u>loose impediment</u> and the ball lie in or touch a <u>hazard</u>, any loose impediment may be removed without penalty. If the ball moves, see Rule 18-2c.

When a player's ball is in motion, a loose impediment on his line of play shall not be removed.

PENALTY FOR BREACH OF RULE:
Match play—Loss of hole; Stroke play—Two strokes.
(Searching for ball in hazard—see Rule 12-1.)
(Touching line of putt—see Rule 16-1a.)

Rule 23 is easy to understand and use so long as you know that loose impediments, according to the Definition, are natural objects

A Bad Break

Because my ball lies in a hazard this twig may not be moved. The same applies to leaves, stones and other loose impediments—all natural objects. In a hazard you can't so much as touch one with your club on your backswing. Of course if the twig were magically changed into a cigar, it could be removed because a cigar is an obstruction—an artificial object. (R. 13-4)

not fixed or growing, not solidly embedded and not adhering to the ball. That's why the relevant Definitions are repeated prior to the actual Rules. There they are instantly accessible.

The prohibition against moving loose impediments in hazards is purposely severe. Generally speaking, when you've hit your ball into a hazard, you've made a mistake and you have to deal with the problem directly. That means not removing leaves or stones that happen to interfere with your stroke.

Following are a sprinkling of Decisions on loose impediments:

● If a stone is partially embedded and may be picked up with ease it is a loose impediment. If there's any doubt, the stone should not be removed.

● A solidly embedded acorn is not a loose impediment. That means you are out of luck when a mower shears off the top of an acorn on your line of putt.

● Plugs of compacted soil, produced in an aerification process, are considered loose impediments.

● One C. Edmund Miller, of Liberty Corner, N.J., once removed leaves just past the hole as his opponent was preparing to putt a frightening downhiller toward a lake. The opponent cried foul. He was right. The opponent has no right to remove loose impediments on the player's line of putt since the line extends beyond the hole.

RULE 24

OBSTRUCTIONS

Definition

An "obstruction" is anything artificial, including the artificial surfaces and sides of roads and paths and manufactured ice, except:

a. Objects defining <u>out of bounds</u>, such as walls, fences, stakes and railings;

b. Any part of an immovable artificial object which is out of bounds; and

c. Any construction declared by the Committee to be an integral part of the course.

24-1

Movable Obstruction

A player may obtain relief from a movable <u>obstruction</u> as follows:

a. If the ball does not lie in or on the obstruction, the obstruction may be removed; if the ball moves, no penalty is incurred and the ball shall be replaced.

b. If the ball lies in or on the obstruction, the ball may be lifted, without penalty, and the obstruction removed. The ball shall <u>through the green</u> or in a <u>hazard</u> be dropped, or on the <u>putting green</u> be placed, as near as possible to the spot directly under the place where the ball lay in or on the obstruction, but not nearer the hole. The ball may be cleaned when lifted under Rule 24-1.

When the ball is in motion, an obstruction on the player's line of play other than an attended flagstick and equipment of the players shall not be removed.

24-2

Immovable Obstruction

a. INTERFERENCE

Interference by an immovable <u>obstruction</u> occurs when a ball lies in or on the obstruction, or so close to the obstruction that the obstruction interferes with the player's <u>stance</u> or the area of his intended swing. If the player's ball lies on the <u>putting green</u>, interference also occurs if an immovable obstruction on the putting green intervenes on his line of putt. Otherwise, intervention on the line of play is not, of itself, interference under this Rule.

b. RELIEF

Except when the ball lies in or touches a <u>water hazard</u> or a <u>lateral water hazard</u>, a player may obtain relief from interference by an immovable <u>obstruction</u>, without penalty, as follows:

(i) *Through the Green:* If the ball lies <u>through the green</u>, the point on the <u>course</u> nearest to where the ball lies shall be determined (without crossing over, through or under the obstruction) which (a) is not nearer the hole, (b) avoids interference (as defined) and (c) is not in a <u>hazard</u> or on a <u>putting green</u>. The player shall lift the ball and drop it within

Movable Obstruction

A rake is artificial and therefore an obstruction. Obviously I want relief. Since this rake can readily be moved, it's a movable obstruction. Since it's movable, I do not have the option of dropping away from the rake without penalty. If the ball was up against the rake and happened to move when I set it aside, I would replace it without penalty. (R. 24-1)

105

one club-length of the point thus determined on ground which fulfills (a), (b) and (c) above.

Note: The prohibition against crossing over, through or under the <u>obstruction</u> does not apply to the artificial surfaces and sides of roads and paths or when the ball lies in or on the obstruction.

    (ii) In a Bunker: If the ball lies in or touches a <u>bunker</u>, the player shall lift and drop the ball in accordance with Clause (i) above, except that the ball must be dropped in the bunker.

    (iii) *On the Putting Green:* If the ball lies on the <u>putting green</u>, the player shall lift the ball and place it in the nearest position to where it lay which affords relief from interference, but not nearer the hole nor in a hazard.

The ball may be cleaned when lifted under Rule 24-2b.

(Ball rolling back into condition from which relief taken—see Rule 20-2c(v).)

    Exception: A player may not obtain relief under Rule 24-2b if (a) it is clearly unreasonable for him to play a stroke because of interference by anything other than an immovable obstruction or (b) interference by an immovable obstruction would occur only through use of an unnecessarily abnormal stance, swing or direction of play.

Note: *If a ball lies in or touches a <u>water hazard</u> (including a <u>lateral water hazard</u>), the player is not entitled to relief with-*

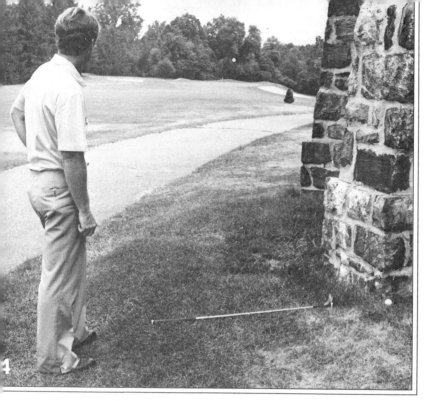

Immovable Obstruction

I'm entitled to relief without penalty in (1) because the stone wall interferes with my stance. The same applies in (2) because now there's interference with my swing. But I get no relief in (3) because the obstruction, although it's on my line, does not interfere with my stance or swing. When you take relief from an immovable obstruction (4), you establish the nearest point, no nearer the hole, where there is no interference, and drop within one club-length of that point.

out penalty from interference by an immovable obstruction. The player shall play the ball as it lies or proceed under Rule 26-1.

PENALTY FOR BREACH OF RULE:
Match play—Loss of hole; Stroke play—Two strokes.

Golfers tend to pounce on the word "relief" with a sense of reckless joy, ignoring the harsh reality that the relief is limited and precise, and is not a *carte blanche* solution to any and every inconvenience caused by artificial objects (obstructions).

First, there are the limitations contained in the Definition, which states that three kinds of artificial objects are *not* obstructions. Therefore, no relief is provided when there is interference by

a. any object used to define out of bounds, including movable objects such as white stakes;

b. any part of an immovable object which is out of bounds;

c. any construction declared by the Committee to be an integral part of the course. The onus is on the Committee to make any such limitation clear on a score card or wherever Local Rules are posted.

Another important limitation in Rule 24 denies relief when an immovable obstruction is on the line of play but is not close enough to interfere with the stance or swing. I'm afraid golfers are misled by what they see on television when "line of sight" relief (dropping to the side of an obstruction on your line) is granted by Local Rule from what are called "temporary immovable obstructions." These include

107

pro-tour necessities such as scoreboards, grandstands and television towers, which are necessarily installed very close to playing areas. There is no such thing as "line of sight" relief in everyday play through the green.

A third limitation has to do with the maximum relief that is available when a ball lies in or on an obstruction, or so close that it interferes with the stance or swing. Rule 24 offers a procedure for finding "the point on the course nearest to where the ball lies" and then allows a drop within one club-length of that point. Neither the point nor the spot at which the ball is dropped can be nearer the hole than the ball's original resting place, in a hazard or on a putting green, yet both must be far enough away so as to avoid the very interference for which the relief is granted. See the illustrations and captions accompanying Rule 24 for an exposition of how to drop away from obstructions.

A fourth limitation denies relief from immovable obstructions when a ball is in a water hazard or lateral water hazard. If your ball is within a water hazard, and there's interference by an immovable obstruction,

Obstructions in Hazards
It's OK to remove obstructions —artificial things—from hazards. Obvious examples include rakes, paper cups and cigarette stubs. If the ball moves in the process you must replace it, but without penalty.

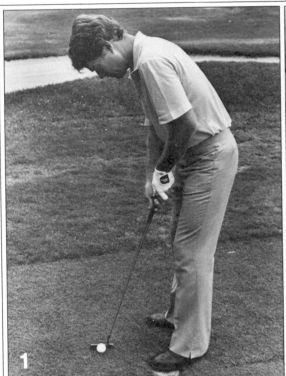

Sprinkler Heads

Since my stance is on a sprinkler head (1), I can take relief without penalty. I've established the nearest point (2) and marked it with a tee. The extent of relief, one club-length, is marked (3) with a second tee. There's another illustration (4) of the new dropping procedure—within the area marked by the tees. When a sprinkler head off a putting green is on your line but does not interfere with your stance or swing (5), there is no free relief. Go ahead and chip the ball. (R. 24-2)

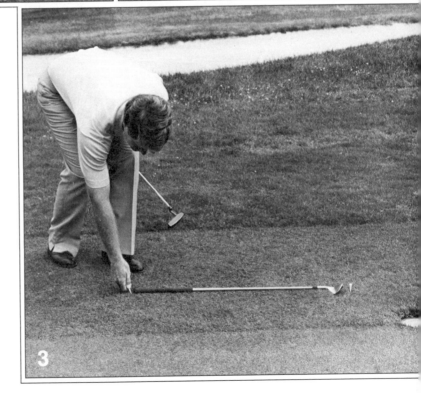

either play it as it lies or drop out of the hazard, with a one-stroke penalty, under Rule 26.

Some other guidelines and cautions in applying Rule 24:

• Whenever the artificial object—for instance a bench—is movable, it may be removed. A player does not have the option of lifting and dropping the ball away from a movable obstruction. That might be to his advantage if the ball lies poorly.

On the other hand, the relief from movable obstructions is generous in that those on the line of play may be removed. Common movable obstructions on the pro tour include gallery stakes, ropes, TV and telephone wires, and various signs.

• Relief from movable obstructions (bottles, cigarette butts, etc.) in hazards is simple. You simply remove them.

• One of the most common obstruction situations arises when the stance or swing is interfered with by wires or ropes supporting young trees. Understand that the relief applies to the wire or rope but not to the tree itself, which means that (a) the "nearest point" must be related to the interfering artificial object and not to the tree, and (b) if the wire or rope doesn't interfere, there is no relief.

• Watch out for sprinkler heads and the plastic caps of irrigation systems located on the aprons of putting greens. The impulse, almost irresistible, is to lift and place the ball off to the side when one of

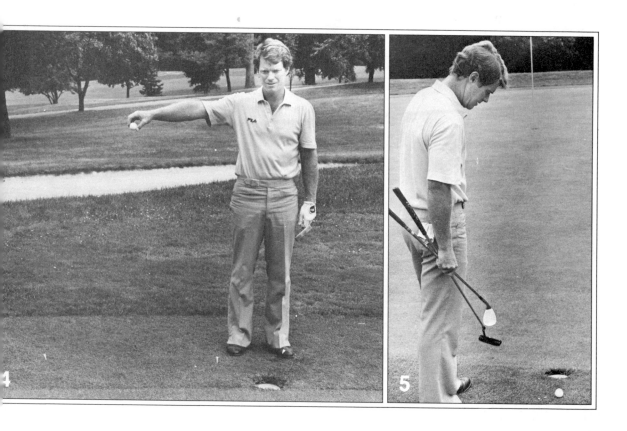

these caps is on your line, especially when your ball is also on the apron and you want to putt it. Fact is, there is no relief. Read it and weep.

Some handy Rule 24 Decisions:

● The player's ball is nestled in a coiled hose—a movable obstruction—but he erroneously treats it as an immovable obstruction and drops away instead of moving the hose.

Answer: The player lifted a ball when he was not entitled to. Under Rule 18-2 he incurs a penalty stroke and has to replace the ball. The player should have moved the hose. If the ball is not replaced it is loss of hole in match play; the penalty expands to two strokes in stroke play.

● A player's ball was four or five inches away from a flat sprinkler head that did not interfere with his stance or swing. The player claimed relief, however, on the ground that the covering constituted a mental hazard.

Answer: He doesn't get it. Mental interference by an obstruction does not entitle the player to relief.

● Is it permissible to drop from an obstruction in the rough into a fairway, if that's where a correct drop might lead you?

1

2

Relief from Cart Paths

An artificially surfaced cart path is an immovable obstruction. I'm entitled to relief even if the ball is off the path, but I have to stand on it (1). Here's how to take relief from the situation shown in (2): I establish the nearest point by sticking in a tee at that point, measure one club-length and mark the width of the area in which I can drop by inserting another tee (3). Then I drop (4) between and behind the tees. There's only one nearest point of relief. In illustration (5) the nearest point is where I'm standing, not where my friend is standing, because the ball is closer to the point on the left. (But if it was closer to the right, you'd have to go to the right—if you want relief— even though the tree poses a problem.) But let's turn it around, imagine that both of us are left-handed players, and the ball is in the same place (6). Now the nearest point shifts over to the right. A key, of course, is that the stance must be taken off the path.

Answer: Yes. There is no distinction in the Rules between fairway and rough; both are covered by the term "through the green."

• A critical interpretation of artificial surfacing holds that a road or path which has been surfaced with anything artificial, *e.g.*, concrete, tar, gravel, wood chips, ash, etc., is an artificially surfaced area and thus an obstruction.

• Irrigation control boxes are often built near the edges of fairways. Is it proper to adopt a Local Rule granting "line of flight" relief?

PAVED
← CART PATH

Dropping from an Obstruction

Three spots might qualify as the nearest point of relief when there's interference by an immovable obstruction, such as a paved cart path.

The point that is the shortest distance from the ball (A) must be used. The three possibilities are behind the obstruction (B); on an arc to the left (C); and on an arc to the right (D). Since line A–B

is shorter than lines A–C and A–D, the nearest point of relief is B. The same principle applies when relief is taken from ground under repair and casual water. (R. 24-2b)

Answer: No, since the boxes are permanent and therefore not analogous to such things as tents and television equipment, which are given special treatment.

● Jack Crist of Charlotte, North Carolina, when Chairman of the USGA Rules of Golf Committee, thought that the term "the point on the course nearest to where the ball lies" needed clarification, when it first appeared in the Rules, and many agreed.

A Decision was published: "When the position of a ball is such that there is interference by an immovable obstruction, there is a specific point on the course (not nearer the hole, nor on the putting green nor in a hazard) nearest to which the ball originally lay at which, if the ball were so positioned, interference would cease to exist. The point is 'the point on the course nearest to where the ball lies.' "

● Then, of course, we have the famous barn door decision which says that a player may open the doors of a barn to enable him to play a shot. The same principle would apply to a ball played from within a clubhouse. It's OK to open a window first because the window is a movable obstruction even though the clubhouse isn't.

"If the ball does not lie in or on an obstruction and an artificially surfaced road or path is not involved, the point in question is the nearest one avoiding interference which can be reached without crossing over, through or under the obstruction.

"In determining the nearest point where interference would cease to exist, the club with which the player would expect to play the next stroke must be used. In measuring the one club-length from the nearest point, the player may use any club selected for the round.

"The prohibition against crossing over, through or under an obstruction does not apply when measuring from the nearest point the one club-length within which the player must drop the ball."

RULE 25

ABNORMAL GROUND CONDITIONS AND WRONG PUTTING GREEN

Definitions

"Casual water" is any temporary accumulation of water on the <u>course</u> which is visible before or after the player takes his <u>stance</u> and is not in a <u>water hazard</u>. Snow and ice are either casual water or <u>loose impediments</u>, at the option of the player, except that manufactured ice is an <u>obstruction</u>. Dew is not casual water.

"Ground under repair" is any portion of the <u>course</u> so marked by order of the Committee or so declared by its authorized representative. It includes material piled for removal and a hole made by a greenkeeper, even if not so marked. Stakes and lines defining ground under repair are in such ground. The margin of ground under repair extends vertically downwards, but not upwards.

Note 1: Grass cuttings and other material left on the course

Casual Water

The ball lies in casual water (1), so I'm entitled to take relief by first determining the nearest point that both avoids the casual water and is not nearer the hole. I haven't reached that point in (2) because my foot is in the water. That's interference. But in (3) I've determined the point and have marked it with a tee. I measure one club-length from that point in (4), lift the club, and—before dropping—I clean the ball (5).

which have been abandoned and are not intended to be re-moved are not ground under repair unless so marked.

Note 2: *The Committee may make a Local Rule prohibiting play from ground under repair.*

a. INTERFERENCE

Interference by <u>casual water</u>, <u>ground under repair</u> or a hole, cast or runway made by a burrowing animal, a reptile or a bird occurs when a ball lies in or touches any of these condi-tions or when the condition interferes with the player's <u>stance</u> or the area of his intended swing.

If the player's ball lies on the <u>putting green</u>, interference also occurs if such condition on the putting green intervenes on his line of putt.

If interference exists, the player may either play the ball as it lies (unless prohibited by Local Rule) or take relief as pro-vided in Clause b.

b. RELIEF

If the player elects to take relief, he shall proceed as fol-lows:

(i) *Through the Green:* If the ball lies <u>through the green</u>,

25-1
Casual Water, Ground Under Repair and Certain Damage to Course

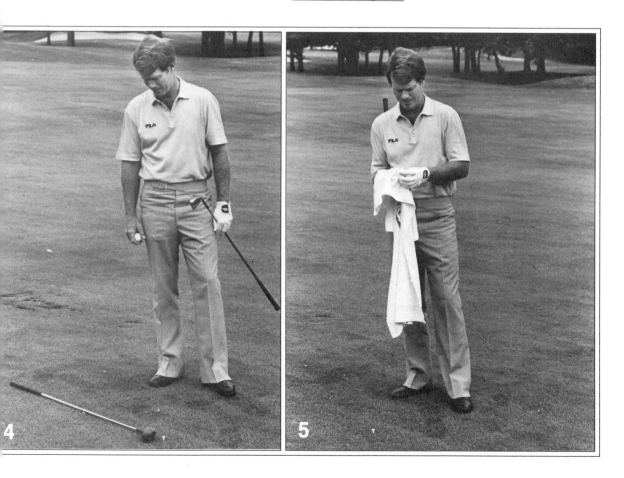

the point on the <u>course</u> nearest to where the ball lies shall be determined which (a) is not nearer the hole, (b) avoids interference by the condition, and (c) is not in a <u>hazard</u> or on a <u>putting green</u>. The player shall lift the ball and drop it without penalty within one club-length of the point thus determined on ground which fulfills (a), (b) and (c) above.

(ii) *In a Hazard:* If the ball lies in or touches a <u>hazard</u>, the player shall lift and drop the ball either:

(a) Without penalty, in the hazard, as near as possible to the spot where the ball lay, but not nearer the hole, on ground which affords maximum available relief from the condition;

or

(b) *Under penalty of one stroke,* outside the hazard, keeping the point where the ball lay directly between the hole and the spot on which the ball is dropped.

Exception: If a ball lies in or touches a <u>water hazard</u> (including a <u>lateral water hazard</u>), the player is not entitled to relief without penalty from a hole, cast or runway made by a burrowing animal, a reptile or a bird. The player shall play the ball as it lies or proceed under Rule 26-1.

(iii) *On the Putting Green:* If the ball lies on the <u>putting green</u>, the player shall lift the ball and place it without penalty in the nearest position to where it lay which affords maximum available relief from the condition, but not nearer the hole nor in a <u>hazard</u>.

The ball may be cleaned when lifted under Rule 25-1b.

(Ball rolling back into condition from which relief taken—see Rule 20-2c(v).)

Exception: A player may not obtain relief under Rule 25-1b if (a) it is clearly unreasonable for him to play a stroke because of interference by anything other than a condition covered by Rule 25-1a or (b) interference by such a condition would occur only through use of an unnecessarily abnormal stance, swing or direction of play.

c. BALL LOST UNDER CONDITION COVERED BY RULE 25-1

It is a question of fact whether a ball lost after having been struck toward a condition covered by Rule 25-1 is lost under such condition. In order to treat the ball as lost under such condition, there must be reasonable evidence to that effect. In the absence of such evidence, the ball must be treated as a lost ball and Rule 27 applies.

(i) *Outside a Hazard*—If a ball is lost outside a <u>hazard</u> under a condition covered by Rule 25-1, the player may take relief as follows: the point on the <u>course</u> nearest to where the ball last crossed the margin of the area shall be determined which (a) is not nearer the hole than where the ball last crossed the margin, (b) avoids interference by the condition and (c) is not in a hazard or on a <u>putting green</u>. He shall drop a ball without penalty within one club-length of the point thus determined on ground which fulfils (a), (b) and (c) above.

(ii) *In a Hazard*—If a ball is lost in a <u>hazard</u> under a condition covered by Rule 25-1, the player may drop a ball either:

(a) Without penalty, in the hazard, as near as possible to the point at which the original ball last crossed the margin of the area, but not nearer the hole, on ground which affords maximum available relief from the condition;

or

(b) *Under penalty of one stroke,* outside the hazard, keeping the point at which the original ball last crossed the margin of the hazard directly between the hole and the spot on which the ball is dropped.

Exception: If a ball lies in a <u>water hazard</u> (including a <u>lateral water hazard</u>), the player is not entitled to relief without penalty for a ball lost in a hole, cast or runway made by a burrowing animal, a reptile or a bird. The player shall proceed under Rule 26-1.

A ball embedded in its own pitch-mark in the ground in any closely mown area <u>through the green</u> may be lifted, cleaned and dropped, without penalty, as near as possible to the spot where it lay but not nearer the hole. "Closely mown area" means any area of the <u>course</u>, including paths through the rough, cut to fairway height or less.

25-2
Embedded Ball

If a ball lies on a <u>putting green</u> other than that of the hole being played, the point on the <u>course</u> nearest to where the ball lies shall be determined which (a) is not nearer the hole and (b) is not in a <u>hazard</u> or on a putting green. The player shall lift the ball and drop it without penalty within one club-length of the point thus determined on ground which fulfills (a) and (b) above. The ball may be cleaned when so lifted.

25-3
Wrong Putting Green

Note: *Unless otherwise prescribed by the Committee, the term "a putting green other than that of the hole being played" includes a practice putting green or pitching green on the course.*

PENALTY FOR BREACH OF RULE:
Match play—Loss of hole; Stroke play—Two strokes.

25-1. Casual Water, Ground Under Repair and Certain Damage to the Course

The word "interference" doesn't always click as it should with readers of the Rules of Golf. "Gets in the way of" or "intervenes" are helpful dictionary definitions. In any event, you are entitled to relief under Rule 25 not only because your ball lies in ground under repair but also if you have to stand in it, even though the ball lies outside the area. The same applies to casual water and burrowing animal holes but not when the animal hole is in a water hazard.

Speaking of burrowing animal holes, a Decision provides the final words on the subject, in reply to a question asking whether relief should be granted from holes made by a dog who digs and leaves behind heaps of earth. "A burrow is a hole or tunnel in the ground made by certain animals, such as rabbits, moles, ground hogs and gophers for shelter and habitation. Thus, a burrowing animal is an animal that makes a hole in which it may live. Since a dog does not dig holes for habitation or shelter, a hole made by a dog is not a burrowing animal hole."

The extent of relief after determining the nearest point is limited to one club-length. The same is true of relief from immovable obstructions under Rule 24.

Determining "the point on the course nearest to where the ball lies"

Ground Under Repair

The relief procedure for ground under repair and casual water are the same. I can take relief if the ball is in ground under repair or if I have to stand in the area. Relief, of course, is optional. If I like the lie, I'll simply play the ball without taking relief. (R. 25-1) is the hardest part of applying Rule 25. It might help to think that there are three possible points to consider every time, but only one of the three is the nearest point in the sense that your ball will have traveled the shortest distance to reach that point. Once you find that point, then you get the additional one-club-length leeway.

Note that on the putting green the relief is liberal, as it allows you to lift, move and *place* the ball to avoid intervention by casual water. However, if the ball is not on the putting green, you can complain, but that's all. Thus, if your ball is just off the green, not interfered with by casual water although there's a puddle on your line, you get no relief.

Remember that there is no such thing, by Definition, as casual water in a water hazard—but there may be casual water in a bunker.

Here are some common ground-under-repair situations:

• A player has a bad lie in ground under repair and wants to drop within the ground under repair.

Answer: He can't do it; he must drop on ground that avoids the condition—that is, outside the ground under repair.

• A player drops outside ground under repair as per Rule 25-1, but the ball rolls back into the ground under repair. It has rolled less than one club-length and no nearer the hole. He likes the lie. May he play?

Answer: No. He must re-drop. (See Rule 20-2c.)

• A player drops outside ground under repair, but now his stance is in the ground under repair. Must he drop again?

Answer: Yes.

• What can a golfer do when a bunker is completely covered by casual water?

Answer: He may drop it in the bunker in the shallowest casual water as near as possible to the spot where the ball first lay, but not nearer the hole or outside the bunker under penalty of one stroke.

• A player's ball lay in the narrow crevice of a tree. A stroke at the ball was a physical impossibility, but when the player took his stance one of his feet was on a burrowing animal hole. Was he entitled to invoke Rule 25?

Answer: No. See Exception to Rule 25-1b which says no relief if the ball's position is such that an attempt to play a stroke would be "clearly unreasonable."

25-2. Embedded Ball

The Rule clearly defines "closely mown area" as cut at fairway height or less. Rule 25-2 does not allow relief for balls embedded in rough. If a Committee feels conditions warrant providing relief for more than "closely mown areas," it is necessary to adopt a Local Rule which might say that relief is granted for any ball embedded through the green, and not just those in "closely mown areas."

25-3. Wrong Putting Green

You may not play from a wrong putting green, including a practice green. The Rule calls for a drop within one club-length of the nearest point, no nearer the hole. This invariably allows for a drop on a beautifully groomed apron, which makes golf-course superintendents wince, but there it is.

RULE 26

WATER HAZARDS (INCLUDING LATERAL WATER HAZARDS)

Definitions

A "water hazard" is any sea, lake, pond, river, ditch, surface drainage ditch or other open water course (whether or not containing water) and anything of a similar nature.

All ground or water within the margin of a water hazard is part of the water hazard. The margin of a water hazard extends vertically upwards and downwards. Stakes and lines defining the margins of water hazards are in the hazards.

Note: *Water hazards (other than lateral water hazards) should be defined by yellow stakes or lines.*

A "lateral water hazard" is a water hazard or that part of a water hazard so situated that it is not possible or is deemed by the Committee to be impracticable to drop a ball behind the water hazard in accordance with Rule 26-1b.

That part of a water hazard to be played as a lateral water hazard should be distinctively marked.

Note: *Lateral water hazards should be defined by red stakes or lines.*

26-1

Ball in Water Hazard

It is a question of fact whether a ball lost after having been struck toward a water hazard is lost inside or outside the hazard. In order to treat the ball as lost in the hazard, there must be reasonable evidence that the ball lodged in it. In the absence of such evidence, the ball must be treated as a lost ball and Rule 27 applies.

If a ball lies in, touches or is lost in a water hazard (whether the ball lies in water or not), the player may *under penalty of one stroke:*

a. Play his next stroke as nearly as possible at the spot from which the original ball was last played (see Rule 20-5);

or

b. Drop a ball behind the water hazard, keeping the point at which the original ball last crossed the margin of the water hazard directly between the hole and the spot on which the ball is dropped, with no limit to how far behind the water hazard the ball may be dropped;

or

c. *As additional options available only if the ball lies in, touches or is lost in a lateral water hazard,* drop a ball outside the water hazard within two club-lengths of (i) the point where the original ball last crossed the margin of the water hazard or (ii) a point on the opposite margin of the water hazard equidistant from the hole. The ball must be dropped and come to rest not nearer the hole than the point where the original ball last crossed the margin of the water hazard.

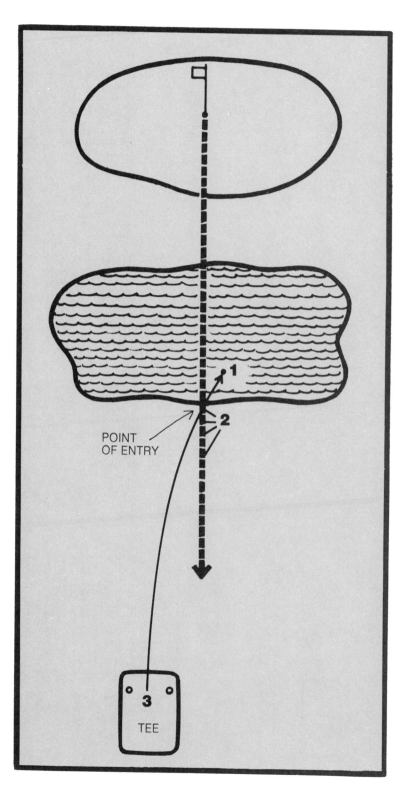

POINT
OF ENTRY

1

2

3

TEE

Water Hazard Options

You can do one of three things when your ball comes to rest in a water hazard: (1) Assuming the ball is playable, go right ahead and play it without penalty. But if it's not playable, imagine a line (2) running from the hole to the point where the ball last crossed the margin of the hazard. You can drop on an extension of that line for a penalty of one stroke. The third option (3) is stroke-and-distance. In this illustration, that means returning to the tee, where your next stroke would be your third. Note that you can't drop along the line of the ball's flight. (R. 26-1)

Lateral Water Hazard Options

There are five options when a ball lies within a lateral water hazard. Three are the same as those for a water hazard: (1) Play the ball as it lies without penalty. (2) Drop behind the hazard on a line formed by the hole and point (A) where the ball entered the hazard with a one-stroke penalty added. (3) Use the stroke-and-distance option. The other two options also call for a penalty stroke. You may drop within two club-lengths of A, no nearer the hole (4) or on the opposite side of the hazard (5). The reference point on the opposite side is B, which is the same distance from the hole as A. (R. 26-1)

LATERAL WATER HAZARD

TEE

124

The ball may be cleaned when lifted under this Rule.
(Ball moving in water in a water hazard—see Rule 14-6.)

a. BALL COMES TO REST IN HAZARD
If a ball played from within a water hazard comes to rest in the hazard after the stroke, the player may:

(i) proceed under Rule 26-1; or

(ii) *under penalty of one stroke,* play his next stroke as nearly as possible at the spot from which the last stroke from outside the hazard was played (see Rule 20-5).

b. BALL LOST OR UNPLAYABLE OUTSIDE HAZARD
  OR OUT OF BOUNDS
If a ball played from within a water hazard is lost or declared unplayable outside the hazard or is out of bounds, the player, after taking *a penalty of one stroke* under Rule 27-1 or 28a, may:

(i) play a ball as nearly as possible at the spot in the hazard from which the original ball was last played (see Rule 20-5); or

(ii) *under an additional penalty of one stroke,* proceed under Rule 26-1b or, if applicable, Rule 26-1c, using as the reference point the point where the original ball last crossed the margin of the hazard before it came to rest in the hazard; or

(iii) *under an additional penalty of one stroke,* play his next stroke as nearly as possible at the spot from which the last stroke from outside the hazard was played (see Rule 20-5).

Note: *If a ball played from within a water hazard is declared unplayable outside the hazard, nothing in Rule 26-2b precludes the player from proceeding under Rule 28b or c.*

PENALTY FOR BREACH OF RULE:
Match play—Loss of hole; Stroke play—Two strokes.

Water hazards and lateral water hazards should be properly marked by yellow or red stakes and lines. When they are not marked there is bound to be confusion. Golfers confronted with unmarked water hazards should complain to the management. It's not that big a deal to install and maintain appropriate markings. Here are some keys to the application of Rule 26:

• When you drop behind a water hazard the ball itself must be dropped on the imaginary line that is formed by the hole and the point where the ball last crossed the margin of the hazard. It doesn't matter where you stand; it's dropping on the line that matters. That's a change. Between 1984 and 1988 the player was permitted to drop an arm's length to either side of the extension of the line which he was required to position himself on.

• When dropping outside a water hazard or lateral water hazard, the options do not include dropping along the "line of flight."

• Fundamental, but worth affirming: If your ball is in the water hazard and can't be found, or it is found and you opt not to play it, the penalty is one stroke. Thus if you drive into a water hazard and drop a ball behind the hazard, your next stroke is your third.

● You may not treat a ball as being lost in a hazard just because it might be in the hazard. There must be "reasonable evidence," which is clarified in a Decision:

"The term 'reasonable evidence' in Rule 26-1 is purposely and necessarily broad so as to permit sensible judgments to be reached on the basis of all the relevant circumstances of particular cases. As applied in this context, a player may not deem his ball lost in a water hazard simply because he thinks the ball may be in the hazard. The evidence must be preponderantly in favor of its being in the hazard. Otherwise, the ball must be considered lost outside the hazard and the player must proceed under Rule 27-1. Physical conditions in the area have a great deal to do with it. For example, if a water hazard is surrounded by a fairway on which a ball could hardly be lost, the existence of reasonable evidence that the ball is in the hazard would be more likely than if there was deep rough in the area. Observing a ball splash in a water hazard would not necessarily provide reasonable evidence, as splashing balls sometimes skip out of hazards."

RULE 27

BALL LOST OR OUT OF BOUNDS; PROVISIONAL BALL

If the original ball is lost under a condition covered by Rule 25-1 (casual water, ground under repair and certain damage to the course), the player may proceed under that Rule. If the original ball is lost in a water hazard, the player shall proceed under Rule 26.

Such Rules may not be used unless there is reasonable evidence that the ball is lost under a condition covered by Rule 25-1 or in a water hazard.

Definitions

A ball is "lost" if:

a. It is not found or identified as his by the player within five minutes after the player's side or his or their caddies have begun to search for it; or

b. The player has put another ball into play under the Rules, even though he may not have searched for the original ball; or

c. The player has played any stroke with a provisional ball from the place where the original ball is likely to be or from a point nearer the hole than that place, whereupon the provisional ball becomes the ball in play.

Time spent in playing a wrong ball is not counted in the five-minute period allowed for search.

"Out of bounds" is ground on which play is prohibited.

When out of bounds is defined by reference to stakes or a fence, or as being beyond stakes or a fence, the out of bounds line is determined by the nearest inside points of the stakes or fence posts at ground level excluding angled supports.

When out of bounds is defined by a line on the ground, the line itself is out of bounds.

The out of bounds line extends vertically upwards and downwards.

A ball is out of bounds when all of it lies out of bounds.

A player may stand out of bounds to play a ball lying within bounds.

A "provisional ball" is a ball played under Rule 27-2 for a ball which may be <u>lost</u> outside a <u>water hazard</u> or may be <u>out of bounds</u>.

If a ball is <u>lost</u> outside a <u>water hazard</u> or is <u>out of bounds</u>, a player shall play a ball, *under penalty of one stroke,* as nearly as possible at the spot from which the original ball was last played (see Rule 20-5).

PENALTY FOR BREACH OF RULE 27-1:
Match play—Loss of hole; Stroke play—Two strokes.

27-1
Ball Lost or Out of Bounds

a. PROCEDURE

If a ball may be <u>lost</u> outside a <u>water hazard</u> or may be <u>out of bounds</u>, to save time the player may play another ball provisionally as nearly as possible at the spot from which the original ball was played (see Rule 20-5). The player shall inform his opponent in match play or his marker or a fellow-competitor in stroke play that he intends to play a <u>provisional ball</u>, and he shall play it before he or his partner goes forward to search for the original ball. If he fails to do so and plays another ball, such ball is not a provisional ball and becomes the <u>ball in play</u> *under penalty of stroke and distance* (Rule 27-1); the original ball is deemed to be lost.

b. WHEN PROVISIONAL BALL BECOMES BALL IN PLAY

The player may play a provisional ball until he reaches the place where the original ball is likely to be. If he plays a stroke with the provisional ball from the place where the original ball is likely to be or from a point nearer the hole than that place, the original ball is deemed to be <u>lost</u> and the provisional ball becomes the ball in play *under penalty of stroke and distance* (Rule 27-1).

If the original ball is lost outside a water hazard or is out of bounds, the provisional ball becomes the ball in play, *under penalty of stroke and distance* (Rule 27-1).

c. WHEN PROVISIONAL BALL TO BE ABANDONED

If the original ball is neither lost outside a water hazard nor out of bounds, the player shall abandon the provisional ball and continue play with the original ball. If he fails to do so, any further strokes played with the provisional ball shall constitute playing a <u>wrong ball</u> and the provisions of Rule 15 shall apply.

Note: *If the original ball lies in a water hazard, the player*

27-2
Provisional Ball

shall play the ball as it lies or proceed under Rule 26. If it is lost in a water hazard or unplayable, the player shall proceed under Rule 26 or 28, whichever is applicable.

Here we have the despised stroke-and-distance penalty, which means that when you knock your tee shot out of bounds (or lose it outside a water hazard), your next stroke is played from the tee again and is your third, not your second. In other words, you not only lose the distance the ball traveled but have to tack on a penalty stroke as well.

Why? Because otherwise an element of farce would be introduced into the game. Everyone agrees that the concept of allowing for the play of a provisional ball for a ball that may be lost or out of bounds is sound in that it saves time and trouble. If the penalty was to be distance only (so that the next stroke from the tee after a ball hit out of bounds counted as the second stroke), we would use the provisional not only as a timesaver but as a "Mulligan," a possible means of getting completely off the hook for playing a bad shot.

Take the par-3 4th hole at the Augusta National Golf Club. It's a hard hole with an impenetrable thicket of cane growth far to the right of the green. If I hit a ball into those canes, I've played an absolutely awful shot. It's not out of bounds and I might have to declare the ball unplayable. There's no way I can make a par and I might well make a 5 or even worse. But suppose Rule 27 were relaxed. Since the ball in the thicket might be lost, I'd be entitled to and would play a provisional ball. Let's say I play this one correctly and knock it eight feet from the hole. I would be tempted not to search for my original ball and instead march right up to the green and have a fifty-fifty chance of salvaging my par. It would be ludicrous for the Rules to allow situations to develop in which it would sometimes be in the player's best interest to lose his ball.

As a matter of fact, the "distance only" penalty was given a try in 1960 by the USGA in what were labeled "Trial Rules." They were quickly abandoned.

All right, you say, but why does it have to be both stroke *and* distance? If a ball goes out of bounds, why not drop a ball within two club-lengths of the point where the ball crossed the boundary instead of having to go all the way back? First of all, it's very hard to determine exactly where a ball goes out of bounds. Moreover, logic demands that the lost ball and out-of-bounds situations may be linked. Wild shots are commonly hit in the direction of boundaries but the ball isn't found. The ball might be out of bounds, but on the other hand it might just as well be lost in the woods on the course. Since there's no way of knowing for sure where the ball is, the only equitable resolution is a Rule in which it doesn't matter whether the ball is out of bounds or lost. Here are what some Decisions have to say about lost balls:

• Once the search for a ball goes beyond five minutes the ball is lost. If a player searches more than five minutes, finds the original and then plays it, he's played a wrong ball. See Rule 15 for a reminder of all the bad things—up to and including disqualification in stroke play —that happen when a wrong ball is played.

• A player refused to identify his ball, unplayable in the woods, after playing a sensational shot with a provisional ball. Q: Is that fair? A: No, it's not. If a player has dishonestly not identified his ball the Committee would be justified in disqualifying that player.

• OK, but suppose the player shanked into the woods on a par-3 hole and knocks his provisional ball within a foot of the hole. The opponent obviously wants there to be a search. The player says, "I think I'll just go up and tap in my provisional for a 4." Q: Has the player, by refusing to search, not dishonestly refused to identify his ball? A: No, not if the player gets to the ball on the green and plays a stroke with it before the original is found by his fleet opponent. But what, you say, about playing out of turn? Sure, he's played out of turn, but all the opponent can do is recall the stroke. That doesn't change the status of the original ball, which was lost once the provisional ball was played from a point nearer the hole than the original ball's position—even out of turn.

27-2. Provisional Ball

Rule 27-2 is a welcome timesaver. Although the language of the Rule seems clear enough, it is often violated by golfers who seem to think they can play provisional balls whenever the original ball might be in any sort of difficulty.

Here are the pitfalls:

• Beware of getting mixed up with water hazards. Let us assume that a ball is driven toward a water hazard flanked by trees and heavy rough. A provisional ball may be played, since the ball may be lost outside the hazard. But if the original ball is found within the hazard, the provisional ball must be abandoned and play continued as if no provisional ball existed.

• Moreover, hear this: If a player plays what he erroneously terms a "provisional ball" from the tee only because his original might be in a water hazard, the second ball from the tee is in play, since it was *not* a provisional ball—*i.e.,* a ball played for a ball that may be lost outside a water hazard or out of bounds.

• When a provisional ball is played because the original may be lost, but the original is found in an unplayable position, the provisional, like it or not, must be abandoned, and play proceeds under Rule 28, which covers unplayable situations.

• Rule 27-2 insists that the player who intends to play a provisional ball announce his intention. If a ball is driven in the direction of a boundary and the unhappy player says nothing or grunts a sound indicating dissatisfaction before driving a second ball, that second ball becomes the ball in play; the original ball, even if it's found on the course, must be abandoned. The player lies 3. The same applies to vague statements such a "I think I better reload," which is not acceptable as an announcement of intention to play a provisional ball.

RULE 28

BALL UNPLAYABLE

The player may declare his ball unplayable at any place on the course except when the ball lies in or touches a <u>water</u>

hazard. The player is the sole judge as to whether his ball is unplayable.

If the player deems his ball to be unplayable, he shall, *under penalty of one stroke:*

a. Play his next stroke as near as possible at the spot from which the original ball was last played (see Rule 20-5); or

b. Drop a ball within two club-lengths of the spot where the ball lay, but not nearer the hole; or

c. Drop a ball behind the point where the ball lay, keeping that point directly between the hole and the spot on which the ball is dropped, with no limit to how far behind that point the ball may be dropped.

If the unplayable ball lies in a bunker and the player elects to proceed under Clause b or c, a ball must be dropped in the bunker.

Unplayable Lie Options

You have three choices when you declare a ball unplayable through the green: (1) Go back and play from the spot where the previous stroke was played, (2) Drop a ball within two club-lengths of the spot where the ball was declared unplayable, no nearer the hole, as shown by the white area, or (3) Imagine a line from the hole to the ball and drop back on an extension of that line. In each instance there's a penalty of one stroke. If the ball is unplayable in a bunker, the stroke-and-distance option (1) is still available. Options 2 and 3, however, are modified to the extent that the ball must be dropped within the bunker if either option is used. Remember that a ball can't be declared unplayable in a water hazard. (R. 28)

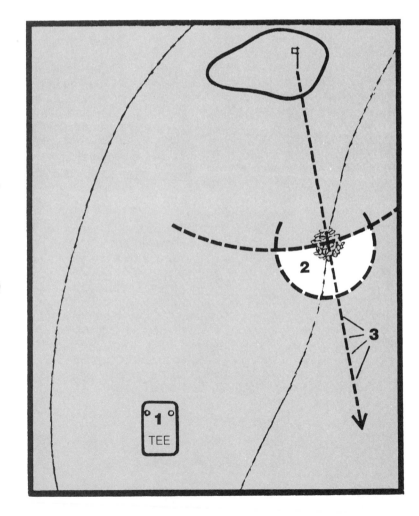

The ball may be cleaned when lifted under this rule.
PENALTY FOR BREACH OF RULE:
Match play—Loss of hole; Stroke play—Two strokes.

The USGA says it gets as much flak on one aspect of Rule 28 as on any other Rule. This seems to result from the general failure to understand that when a ball in a bunker is declared unplayable, the player may avail himself of the stroke-and-distance penalty. The ball may indeed be removed from the bunker and returned to the spot from which the ball was played into the bunker. You can *always* invoke the stroke-and-distance penalty.

Rule 28 Decisions include these:

• A player's ball bounced off a rock and rebounded behind him in the woods. He declared it unplayable and elected to drop at the original lie. His opponent protested, claiming that the player was advancing the ball toward the hole without playing a stroke. Who was right?

Answer: The player was entitled to drop at the original lie under the "stroke and distance" option, even though, in this rare instance, he gained rather than lost distance.

• How do you proceed when a ball is unplayable in a tree?

Answer: You determine the spot directly beneath the ball in the tree and then use Rule 28 just as if the ball were unplayable on the ground at that spot.

• A ball dropped from an unplayable lie into *another* unplayable lie is in play, so be careful. The same principle applies when you drop away from a cart path and the drop results in an unplayable lie. You don't get to do it over without penalty. Moral: Know what you are doing before you pick a ball up and drop it.

OTHER FORMS OF PLAY

RULE 29

THREESOMES AND FOURSOMES

Definitions

Threesome: A match in which one plays against two, and each side plays one ball.

Foursome: A match in which two play against two, and each side plays one ball.

29-1
General

In a threesome or a foursome, during any <u>stipulated round</u> the partners shall play alternately from the teeing grounds and alternately during the play of each hole. <u>Penalty strokes</u> do not affect the order of play.

29-2
Match Play

If a player plays when his partner should have played, *his side shall lose the hole.*

29-3
Stroke Play

If the partners play a stroke or strokes in incorrect order, such stroke or strokes shall be canceled and *the side shall incur a penalty of two strokes.* The side shall correct the error by playing a ball in correct order at the spot from which it first played in incorrect order (see Rule 20-5). If the side plays a stroke from the next <u>teeing ground</u> without first correcting the error or, in the case of the last hole of the round, leaves the <u>putting green</u> without declaring its intention to correct the error, *the side shall be disqualified.*

Rule 29 is almost never referred to in the United States, because a threesome is virtually an extinct form of play and we very seldom play foursomes.

Remember what the Definition says: a threesome is not what happens when three golfers play together. It's a form of play in which one plays against two, and each side plays one ball; that is, the team of two plays alternate strokes with one ball. A foursome is not what happens when four golfers play together; it's a form of competition in which two play against two with each side using one ball, playing alternate strokes.

At the great Muirfield Course in Scotland, home of the Honourable Company of Edinburgh Golfers, there's a venerable tradition concerning foursomes which I think should be tried, at least occasionally, at American clubs.

At Muirfield nothing except foursomes play is permitted on weekend mornings. A brisk foursome, which might have one partner already in the drive zones on many holes waiting to play the second shot for his team, can be played in two and a half hours.

Then comes lunch, and perhaps a four-ball match played in another three and a half hours. All told, the member gets in 36 holes and lunch (with a stupefying drink named Kümmel) in less than seven hours—an estimable goal for all of us.

RULE 30

THREE-BALL, BEST-BALL AND FOUR-BALL MATCH PLAY

Three-Ball: A match play competition in which three play against one another, each playing his own ball. Each player is playing two distinct matches.

Best-Ball: A match in which one plays against the better ball of two or the best ball of three players.

Four-Ball: A match in which two play their better ball against the better ball of two other players.

The Rules of Golf, so far as they are not at variance with the following special Rules, shall apply to three-ball, best-ball and four-ball matches.

30-1
Rules of Golf Apply

a. BALL AT REST MOVED BY AN OPPONENT
Except as otherwise provided in the Rules, if the player's ball is touched or moved by an opponent, his <u>caddie</u> or <u>equipment</u> other than during search, Rule 18-3b applies. *That opponent shall incur a penalty stroke in his match with the player,* but not in his match with the other opponent.

b. BALL DEFLECTED OR STOPPED BY AN OPPONENT ACCIDENTALLY
If a player's ball is accidentally deflected or stopped by an opponent, his <u>caddie</u> or <u>equipment</u>, no penalty shall be incurred. In his match with that opponent the player may play the ball as it lies or, before another stroke is played by either

30-2
Three-Ball Match Play

133

side, he may cancel the stroke and replay it (see Rule 20-5). In his match with the other opponent, the ball shall be played as it lies.

Exception: Ball striking person attending flagstick—see Rule 17-3b.

(Ball purposely deflected or stopped by opponent—see Rule 1-2.)

30-3
Best-Ball and Four-Ball Match Play

a. REPRESENTATION OF SIDE

A side may be represented by one partner for all or any part of a match; all partners need not be present. An absent partner may join a match between holes, but not during play of a hole.

b. MAXIMUM OF FOURTEEN CLUBS

The side shall be penalized for a breach of Rule 4-4 by any partner.

c. ORDER OF PLAY

Balls belonging to the same side may be played in the order the side considers best.

d. WRONG BALL

If a player plays a stroke with a <u>wrong ball</u> except in a <u>hazard,</u> *he shall be disqualified for that hole,* but his partner incurs no penalty even if the wrong ball belongs to him. The owner of the ball shall replace it on the spot from which it was played, without penalty. If the ball is not immediately recoverable, another ball may be substituted.

e. DISQUALIFICATION OF SIDE

(i) *A side shall be disqualified* for a breach of any of the following by any partner:

Rule 1-3—Agreement to Waive Rules.
Rule 4-1, -2 or -3—Clubs.
Rule 5-1 or -2—The Ball.
Rule 6-2a—Handicap (playing off higher handicap).
Rule 6-4—Caddie.
Rule 6-7—Undue Delay (repeated offense).
Rule 14-3—Artificial Devices and Unusual Equipment.

(ii) *A side shall be disqualified* for a breach of any of the following by all partners:

Rule 6-3—Time of Starting and Groups.
Rule 6-8—Discontinuance of Play.

f. EFFECT OF OTHER PENALTIES

If a player's breach of a Rule assists his partner's play or adversely effects an opponent's play, *the partner incurs the applicable penalty in addition to any penalty incurred by the player.*

In all other cases where a player incurs a penalty for breach of a Rule, the penalty shall not apply to his partner. Where the penalty is stated to be loss of hole, the effect shall be to disqualify the player for that hole.

g. ANOTHER FORM OF MATCH PLAYED CONCURRENTLY

In a best-ball or four-ball match when another form of

match is played concurrently, the above special Rules shall apply.

The most popular form of play is undoubtedly four-ball match play, which consists of two playing their better ball on each hole against the better ball of two others.

Rule 30 also covers Best-Ball (when one player goes up against the best ball of either two or three others) and Three-Ball (when three play against one another, each playing his own ball). But these two forms of play are so rare that we'll skip them and concentrate on four-ball match play.

Let's go right to the site of common confusion—on the putting green: In four-ball match, good old A and B are up against C and D.

CASE 1: A is away and B's ball is inches beyond the hole in such a position that it might very well assist A as a backstop. Mr. A would like B's ball to stay right where it is, but back in Rule 22 we learned that C and D have the right to require that B's ball be lifted.

CASE 2: This time B's ball is directly in front of the hole on A's line. Naturally, A and B want B's ball lifted and they may do so.

CASE 3: Now picture C's ball just beyond the hole where it might help A. C can mark and lift his ball.

CASE 4: C's ball is on A's line. A can require him to lift it.

Let's assume, however, that in each case no ball is marked, that A putts and strikes the ball of either B, his partner, or C, his opponent. There is no penalty. Mr. A plays from where his ball then lies. The owner of the ball moved, be it partner or opponent, must replace his ball.

Singles matches are often played concurrently with the four-ball match. Thus A and B are not only going up against the team of C and D, but A is waging singles matches at the same time against C and D, and sometimes even against partner B. What to do when the procedure for four-ball match play is at variance with those for single matches? Easy. The four-ball Rules have priority! It says so loud and clear in Rule 30-3g.

Some other key elements in four-ball matches:

• Rule 30-3c introduces a strategic possiblity in that even though A is away, his partner—Dr. B—may play first. Then it's A's turn.

• When your ball is deflected by your partner, caddie or equipment (including a cart you may be sharing), you are disqualified for that hole, but your partner is not.

• When your ball is accidentally deflected by one of your opponents, their caddies or their equipment, there is no penalty. You have a choice of either playing your ball as it lies or replaying the stroke.

• When a player violates a Rule, his partner is not penalized unless the nature of the violation is such that it helps his partner or hurts the play of an opponent. When that happens, both members of the team are penalized. Example: After balls have been lifted and replaced on a putting green, A makes a mistake and putts from the spot where B's marker was. The putt is a tricky downhiller, with a big right-to-left break. A, having played from the wrong place, is disqualified on that hole, and B, since he might very well have been assisted by observing the roll of the ball, should also be disqualified.

Four-Ball Match Play

In a four-ball match, any player can have any ball lifted before a stroke is made. In this illustration, A and B are partners and it's A's turn to putt. He'll surely require that C's ball be lifted, since it's on his line. A would probably like B's ball to stay right where it is, since it could serve as a useful backstop, but either C or D can require B to lift his ball. As for ball D, it's off the line of putt, but A can have it lifted if it bothers him. If any ball is not lifted and is struck by ball A, there is no penalty. A would play from where his ball then lies, while the owner of the displaced ball, whether he's A's partner or opponent, must replace it. (R. 30)

If one partner is late, or even if he never shows up, his partner alone can play the other team. If the missing partner shows up, he can join the match in progress, but only at the start of any hole.

RULE 31

FOUR-BALL STROKE PLAY

In four-ball stroke play two competitors play as partners, each playing his own ball. The lower score of the partners is the score for the hole. If one partner fails to complete the play of a hole, there is no penalty.

The Rules of Golf, so far as they are not at variance with the following special rules, shall apply to four-ball stroke play.

31-1
Rules of Golf Apply

A side may be represented by either partner for all or any part of a stipulated round; both partners need not be present. An absent competitor may join his partner between holes, but not during play of a hole.

31-2
Representation of Side

The side shall be penalized for a breach of Rule 4-4 by either partner.

31-3
Maximum of Fourteen Clubs

The marker is required to record for each hole only the gross score of whichever partner's score is to count. The gross scores to count must be individually identifiable; otherwise *the side shall be disqualified.* Only one of the partners need be responsible for complying with Rule 6-6b.
(Wrong score—see Rule 31-7a.)

31-4
Scoring

Balls belonging to the same side may be played in the order the side considers best.

31-5
Order of Play

If a competitor plays a stroke with a wrong ball except in a hazard, *he shall add two penalty strokes to his score for the hole* and shall then play the correct ball. His partner incurs no penalty even if the wrong ball belongs to him.
The owner of the ball shall replace it on the spot from which it was played, without penalty. If the ball is not immediately recoverable, another ball may be substituted.

31-6
Wrong Ball

a. BREACH BY ONE PARTNER
A side shall be disqualified from the competition for a breach of any of the following by either partner:
Rule 1-3—Agreement to Waive Rules.

31-7
Disqualification Penalties

137

Rule 3-4—Refusal to Comply with Rule.

Rule 4-1, -2 or -3—Clubs.

Rule 5-1 or -2—The Ball.

Rule 6-2b—Handicap (playing off higher handicap; failure to record handicap).

Rule 6-4—Caddie.

Rule 6-6b—Signing and Returning Card.

Rule 6-6d—Wrong Score for Hole, *i.e.,* when the recorded lower score of the partners is lower than actually taken. If the recorded lower score of the partners is higher than actually taken, it must stand as returned.

Rule 6-7—Undue Delay (repeated offense).

Rule 7-1—Practice Before or Between Rounds.

Rule 14-3—Artificial Devices and Unusual Equipment.

Rule 31-4—Gross Scores to Count Not Individually Identifiable.

b. Breach by Both Partners

A side shall be disqualified:

(i) for a breach by both partners of Rule 6-3 (Time of Starting and Groups) or Rule 6-8 (Discontinuance of Play), or

(ii) if, at the same hole, each partner is in breach of a Rule the penalty for which is disqualification from the competition or for a hole.

c. For the Hole Only

In all other cases where a breach of a Rule would entail disqualification, *the competitor shall be disqualfied only for the hole at which the breach occurred.*

31-8
Effect of Other Penalties

If a competitor's breach of a Rule assists his partner's play, *the partner incurs the applicable penalty in addition to any penalty incurred by the competitor.*

In all other cases where a competitor incurs a penalty for breach of a Rule, the penalty shall not apply to his partner.

The Rules governing four-ball stroke and four-ball match play differ when a ball is moved by another ball. In four-ball stroke play, when a ball is putted from the putting green and strikes another ball on the green, the player who putted is penalized two strokes. The moved ball must be replaced.

Partners in four-ball stroke play may not "use" each other's balls as potential backstops. If A is about to play from a bunker and the ball of partner B is just beyond the hole, B's ball should be removed.

A and B should handle this detail by themselves, but if they are careless, the fellow-competitors, C and D, should have B's ball lifted —in fairness to the rest of the field.

Rule 31 is customarily adopted to control best-ball-of-four competitions—those in which each four-man team counts the best score on a hole as the team score for the hole. Another standard variation is the pro-amateur format, which finds the pro recording his score on each hole (since he's playing a stroke play competition against the other pros in the field) while at the same time engaging his amateur partners in a best-ball-of-four (or even five) competition.

RULE 32

BOGEY, PAR AND STABLEFORD COMPETITIONS

Bogey, par and Stableford competitions are forms of stroke competition in which play is against a fixed score at each hole. The rules for stroke play, so far as they are not at variance with the following special Rules, apply.

a. BOGEY AND PAR COMPETITIONS

The reckoning for bogey and par competitions is made as in match play. Any hole for which a competitor makes no return shall be regarded as a loss. The winner is the competitor who is most successful in the aggregate of holes.

The marker is responsible for marking only the gross number of strokes for each hole where the competitor makes a net score equal to or less than the fixed score.

Note: *Maximum of 14 clubs—Penalties as in match play— see Rule 4-4.*

b. STABLEFORD COMPETITIONS

The reckoning in Stableford competitions is made by points awarded in relation to a fixed score at each hole as follows:

Hole Played in	Points
More than one over fixed score or no score returned	0
One over fixed score	1
Fixed score	2
One under fixed score	3
Two under fixed score	4
Three under fixed score	5

The winner is the competitor who scores the highest number of points.

The marker shall be responsible for marking only the gross number of strokes at each hole where the competitor's net score earns one or more points.

Note: *Maximum of 14 clubs (Rule 4-4)—Penalties applied as follows: From total points scored for the round, deduction of two points for each hole at which any breach occurred; maximum deduction per round: four points.*

a. FROM THE COMPETITION

A competitor shall be disqualified from the competition for a breach of any of the following:

Rule 1-3—Agreement to Waive Rules.
Rule 3-4—Refusal to Comply with Rule.

Rule 4-1, -2 or -3—Clubs.
Rule 5-1 or -2—The Ball.
Rule 6-2b—Handicap (playing off higher handicap; failure to record handicap).
Rule 6-3—Time of Starting and Groups.
Rule 6-4—Caddie.
Rule 6-6b—Signing and Returning Card.
Rule 6-6d—Wrong Score for Hole, except that no penalty shall be incurred when a breach of this Rule does not affect the result of the hole.
Rule 6-7—Undue Delay (repeated offense).
Rule 6-8—Discontinuance of Play.
Rule 7-1—Practice Before or Between Rounds.
Rule 14-3—Artificial Devices and Unusual Equipment.

b. For a Hole

In all other cases where a breach of a Rule would entail disqualification, *the competitor shall be disqualified only for the hole at which the breach occurred.*

Rule 32 sets down the conditions for some forms of competition that offer a form of relief from the routine of standard stroke play.

Bogey or par competitions are played against a fixed score. The most popular method calls for the par on each hole to serve as the opponent. A player competes against par with the help of a handicap. The winner is the player who is most ahead of par after eighteen holes.

Stableford competitions are indigenous to Great Britain. They're often called "point" tournaments here. They're a lot of fun because they allow players of every level of skill to play, suffer and exult together. A common form of Stableford sends out teams of four, each player using full handicap. A net score of a double bogey, or worse, for a player earns no point on a hole, but a bogey is worth 1 point, a par 2 points and so on up to 5 points on a hole for a net double eagle. The winning team is the one that amasses the most total points. Every two-foot putt for a net bogey takes on a meaning all its own.

Stableford, in case you're interested, was Dr. Frank B. Stableford of Great Britain, a surgeon and first-rate golfer who invented the scoring system that bears his name. History records that the first Stableford tournament was played on May 16, 1932, on the Wallasey Links, Cheshire, England.

ADMINISTRATION

RULE 33

THE COMMITTEE

The Committee shall lay down the conditions under which a competition is to be played.

The Committee has no power to waive a Rule of Golf.

Certain special Rules governing stroke play are so substantially different from those governing match play that combining the two forms of play is not practicable and is not permitted. The results of matches played and the scores returned in these circumstances shall not be accepted.

In stroke play the Committee may limit a referee's duties.

a. DEFINING BOUNDS AND MARGINS
The Committee shall define accurately:
  (i) the course and out of bounds,
  (ii) the margins of water hazards and lateral water hazards,
  (iii) ground under repair, and
  (iv) obstructions and integral parts of the course.
b. NEW HOLES
New holes should be made on the day on which a stroke competition begins and at such other times as the Committee considers necessary, provided all competitors in a single round play with each hole cut in the same position.
Exception: When it is impossible for a damaged hole to be repaired so that it conforms with the Definition, the Committee may make a new hole in a nearby similar position.
c. PRACTICE GROUND
Where there is no practice ground available outside the area of a competition course, the Committee should lay down the area on which players may practice on any day of a competition, if it is practicable to do so. On any day of a stroke competition, the Committee should not normally permit prac-

33-1
Conditions: Waiving Rule

33-2
The Course

141

tice on or to a <u>putting green</u> or from a <u>hazard</u> of the competition course.

d. COURSE UNPLAYABLE

If the Committee or its authorized representative considers that for any reason the course is not in a playable condition or that there are circumstances which render the proper playing of the game impossible, it may, in match play or stroke play, order a temporary suspension of play or, in stroke play, declare play null and void and cancel all scores for the round in question. When play has been temporarily suspended, it shall be resumed from where it was discontinued, even though resumption occurs on a subsequent day. When a round is canceled, all penalties incurred in that round are canceled.

(Procedure in discontinuing play—see Rule 6-8.)

33-3
Times of Starting and Groups

The Committee shall lay down the times of starting and, in stroke play, arrange the groups in which competitors shall play.

When a match play competition is played over an extended period, the Committee shall lay down the limit of time within which each round shall be completed. When players are allowed to arrange the date of their match within these limits, the Committee should announce that the match must be played at a stated time on the last day of the period unless the players agree to a prior date.

33-4
Handicap Stroke Table

The Committee shall publish a table indicating the order of holes at which handicap strokes are to be given or received.

33-5
Score Card

In stroke play, the Committee shall issue for each competitor a score card containing the date and the competitor's name or, in foursome or four-ball stroke play, the competitors' names.

In stroke play, the Committee is responsible for the addition of scores and application of the handicap recorded on the card.

In four-ball stroke play, the Committee is responsible for recording the better-ball score for each hole and in the process applying the handicaps recorded on the card, and adding the better-ball scores.

In bogey, par and Stableford competitions, the Committee is responsible for applying the handicap recorded on the card and determining the result of each hole and the overall result or points total.

33-6
Decision of Ties

The Committee shall announce the manner, day and time for the decision of a halved match or of a tie, whether played on level terms or under handicap.

A halved match shall not be decided by stroke play. A tie in stroke play shall not be decided by a match.

A penalty of disqualification may in exceptional individual cases be waived, modified or imposed if the Committee considers such action warranted.

Disqualification Penalty; Committee Discretion

a. POLICY

The Committee may make and publish Local Rules for abnormal conditions if they are consistent with the policy of the Governing Authority for the country concerned as set forth in Appendix I to these Rules.

b. WAIVING PENALTY

A penalty imposed by a Rule of Golf shall not be waived by a Local Rule.

Local Rules

Rule 33 is addressed to those in charge of a competition—the Committee—rather than to the player, but it behooves every golfer to know what Rule 33 is all about. Those who serve on Committees at any level of play should know it inside out. Here's an analysis of each part of Rule 33.

33-1. Conditions: Waiving Rule

The conditions should be spelled out in the finest detail. They include the form of play, who is eligible to enter, the number of players in the field, the schedule of rounds, and prizes.

The third paragraph points out that match and stroke play are like oil and water. Golfers nevertheless go right on attempting to play matches during a stroke-play round. They run up against conflicts such as the elementary one that occurs when a ball not "away" is played. In match play, the opponent can recall that stroke; in stroke play, there is no penalty.

33-2. The Course

It's the responsibility of Committees to keep courses marked properly for everyday play—particularly with respect to the margins of water hazards and ground under repair. The effort should be made.

When water hazards are not defined and players have to sort things out for themselves, they should bear in mind that the natural limit of the hazard is considered the spot where the ground breaks down to form the depression containing the water. That's where lines and stakes defining the limits of water hazards should normally be placed.

The Committee's powers and limitations with respect to suspending play or canceling a round are spelled out in Rule 33-2d.

In match play, all a Committee can do is suspend play and decide when play is to be resumed. Once a match starts and the course becomes unplayable, the results of the holes played before suspension of play are to stand as recorded. Any strokes taken on a hole not completed count. Play is resumed where the ball lay at the time of suspension. The match is never begun anew on the first tee.

In stroke play the Committee can, at its discretion, either cancel an entire round or rule that play is to be resumed where it was discontinued—even on a later day. As a general rule of thumb, the USGA thinks that it's reasonable for a Committee to cancel an entire round when

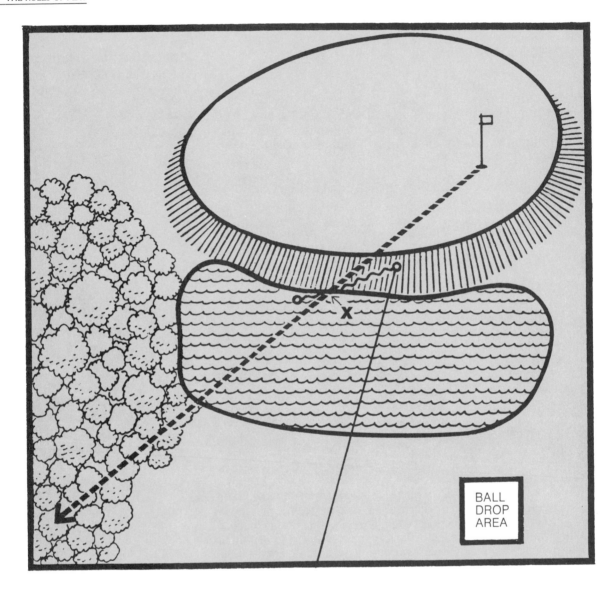

BALL
DROP
AREA

Ball-Drop Areas

Committees can install special ball-drop areas when it's impractical or unfair to limit players to the standard water hazard options. Take this hole, which has a pond directly in front of the green and a slope between the pond and the elevated green. Balls often carry beyond the hazard into the slope but then carom back into the hazard. Often dropping behind the point where the ball last entered the hazard (X) on an extension of a line between the point and the hole means the player would have to drop into a veritable jungle. The stroke-and-distance option, of course, is always available, but that seems too severe. So the Committee installs a clearly defined ball-drop area (lower right), which the player may use for the customary penalty of one stroke.

less than half the field completes or could complete play on the day in question. On the PGA Tour, our Committee seldom cancels a round once play has started. The point is that Committees are all-powerful in this regard, and they have different priorities. What's best for the Tour, where it's very important to complete 72 holes by Sunday because of travel schedules, may not be best for a club member-guest tournament.

33-3. Times of Starting and Groups

Club match-play competitions are often fouled up by a failure of Committees to specify and enforce time limits for the play of rounds. The inability or unwillingness of opponents to get together for a match can spoil a tournament. One way to forestall such a delay is to assign starting times in advance to every match in every round but to allow any match to be played at another time, or even on another day, provided the match is completed prior to the time and date established for the next round.

33-4. Handicap Stroke Table

The order in which handicap strokes are allocated appears on all club score cards. Clubs agonize over the order in which strokes should be allocated, but USGA mathematicians have run computer studies suggesting that it makes little or no difference over the long run on which holes the strokes are taken. What matters is that the total number of strokes between opponents be equitable.

33-5. Score Card

Score cards are required only in stroke play. In match play they are a convenience, but all that matters is that the opponents agree on the status and conclusion of the match. They are not required to sign or return a card.

The Committee bears the responsibility for addition. The player has to put in the correct numbers for each hole. If a player does his job but then fouls up the addition, he is not to worry. The Committee has to get it right.

33-6. Decision of Ties

Committees often fail to announce in advance what will happen in the event of a tie. Whenever they fail to do so, someone is invariably unhappy because the method selected after the fact always seems to favor someone else.

33-7. Disqualification Penalty; Committee Discretion

Let's take a couple of examples of what this section means:

• As a condition of play, a Committee says it's OK to tamp down something it calls "spike marks." In doing so, it has waived Rule 16-1. Boo and hiss! The game is now being played under something other than the Rules of Golf.

• Rule 6-3a says that a player is to be disqualified if he arrives at the first tee late. But suppose he's about to turn into the club driveway and sees a fire in a house across the street. He stops, runs into the building and saves a child, a dog and the kid's stereo. Then he re-

145

sumes his journey but shows up ten minutes late. The Committee should certainly consider waiving any penalty.

33-8. Local Rules

Before any round, the wise golfer will check the back of the score card and any other likely place, such as a bulletin board, for the posting of Local Rules. A Committee should not impose Local Rules contrary to the Rules of Golf. One bad example would be a Local Rule reading "fourteen-club rule waived."

RULE 34

DISPUTES AND DECISIONS

34-1

Claims and Penalties

a. MATCH PLAY

In match play if a claim is lodged with the Committee under Rule 2-5, a decision should be given as soon as possible so that the state of the match may, if necessary, be adjusted.

If a claim is not made within the time limit provided by Rule 2-5, it shall not be considered unless it is based on facts previously unknown to the player making the claim and the player making the claim had been given wrong information (Rules 6-2a and 9) by an opponent. In any case, no later claim shall be considered after the result of the match has been officially announced, unless the Committee is satisfied that the opponent knew he was giving wrong information.

b. STROKE PLAY

Except as provided below, in stroke play no penalty shall be rescinded, modified or imposed after the competition is closed. A competition is deemed to have closed when the result has been officially announced or, in stroke play qualifying followed by match play, when the player has teed off in his first match.

A penalty of disqualification shall be imposed at any time if a competitor:

(i) returns a score for any hole lower than actually taken (Rule 6-6d) for any reason other than failure to include a penalty which he did not know he had incurred; or

(ii) returns a score card on which he has recorded a handicap which he knows is higher than that to which he is entitled, and this affects the number of strokes received (Rule 6-2b).

34-2

Referee's Decision

If a referee has been appointed by the Committee, his decision shall be final.

34-3

146 **Committee's Decision**

In the absence of a referee, the players shall refer any dispute to the Committee, whose decision shall be final.

If the Committee cannot come to a decision, it shall refer

the dispute to the Rules of Golf Committee of the United States Golf Association, whose decision shall be final.

If the point in doubt or dispute has not been referred to the Rules of Golf Committee, the player or players have the right to refer an agreed statement through the Secretary of the Club to the Rules of Golf Committee for an opinion as to the correctness of the decision given. The reply will be sent to the Secretary of the Club or Clubs concerned.

If play is conducted other than in accordance with the Rules of Golf, the Rules of Golf Committee will not give a decision on any question.

Rule 34 covers the sensitive areas of doubts and disagreements and tells how to settle them. Each of its sections deserves careful consideration.

34-1. Claims and Penalties

Focus on the words "claim" and on "wrong information."

A claim, while there are nice and not-so-nice ways of going about it, boils down to telling your opponent that you think he has violated a Rule. In order for a claim to be valid, it must be timely. It's no good seeing him ground his club in a hazard on the 12th hole and bringing up the painful subject when you're 1 down playing the 18th. You see, the statute of limitations for the 12th hole expired when one of you drove from the 13th tee, since you witnessed the violation.

Wrong information usually has to do with the number of strokes taken. It applies to a bald-faced lie (having taken seven strokes but saying you've taken only six) and, in an application that goes right to the heart of the game, it applies even if you were not aware of the violation.

Some landmark decisions on claims:

• A pushed his tee shot into the rough and among trees on the 8th hole. After searching for three or four minutes, he found a ball on the adjoining 9th fairway. It was the same make and number as his ball. A played it and went on to win the 8th hole. After they began to play the 9th hole, a player in the group ahead of them informed A that he had played the wrong ball on the 8th hole. After examining the ball again, A discovered that he had indeed played a wrong ball. Could B claim the 8th hole retroactively?

Answer: Yes, he could. A had given wrong information by failing to inform his opponent of the violation, even though A was not aware he had played a wrong ball. This would apply anytime until the result of the match is officially announced. In club play, that means when the winner's name is posted on a score sheet.

• With his opponent B safely on in 2, A takes 3 strokes to get out of a bunker and concedes the hole. As B picks up his ball, he realizes and announces that he played a wrong ball during the play of the hole. A, although he had conceded, claims the hole.

Answer: A's claim is valid, since it was made before either player played from the next tee. He wins the hole.

• Does a player calling a violation on a hole have to cite the Rule violated, or is it good enough that he knows some Rule has been violated?

Answer: The claim must be reasonably specific and accurate, but the player calling the hole doesn't have to know the Rule's number. For instance, if A putts straddle- or croquet-style and B says "The Rules prohibit such a stance and I call the hole," the Committee should uphold the claim. But if B had said "I call the hole because a stroke from your stance is automatically a push," the claim should not be upheld, since a straddle-style stroke is not automatically a push.

Some stroke play incidents, under 34-1b:

On the morning after the 1977 Jackie Gleason Inverrary Classic ended, Hale Irwin was jolted by a newspaper account of the final round. He read that Grier Jones had been penalized for dropping into a special "ball drop" area after hitting his ball into a water hazard. The Local Rule that applied to the situation said the drop area could be used only if a ball entered the hazard in a particular area. Jones had misunderstood the Rule and used the drop area even though he was not entitled to use it. Irwin realized he had done exactly the same thing. He had failed to include a two-stroke penalty on the hole in question, he had turned in a score lower than the one he actually made and he should be disqualified. He had tied for seventh and his prize was $7,375.

Irwin called Clyde Mangum, Deputy Commissioner of Tour Operations, and in effect turned himself in. He told Mangum of his error and said he considered himself disqualified and would return his check forthwith. Mangum replied that Irwin could not be penalized after the results of the tournament had been announced, since wrong information had not been given knowingly. He hadn't *knowingly* violated a Rule. Irwin was adamant. Mangum said he would not accept the check, and suggested that they call the ultimate USGA Rules expert, P. J. Boatwright, who, as Mangum knew he would, told Irwin that it would be contrary to the Rules of Golf for any penalty to be invoked at that point.

If the incident had occurred *between* rounds, while the tournament was still in progress, Irwin would have been disqualified under Rule 6-6, for returning a score lower than he'd actually made. The point behind this Rule is that there must be a time when a competition is finished. Irwin happened to learn of the violation the day after it happened, but he might just as easily have learned of it on a practice putting green with Grier Jones six months later. Without a statute of limitations we'd never be certain of the outcome of a tournament.

34-2. Referee's Decision

The only time I play with a referee is when I'm in contention in the last rounds of either the U.S. or British Open Championship, the PGA Championship, or the Ryder Cup Match. In those events, referees are customarily appointed to accompany the final pairings. All my other competitive rounds are administered by representatives of the Committee (in my case the PGA Tour staff) sprinkled around the course and ready to help when needed.

34-3. Committee's Decision

Dozens of times every year, written replies to Rules questions from the USGA begin with these ominous words: "The Committee's decision was wrong. However, it was final under Rule 34-3."

It has to be that way. Someone has to be in charge to make rulings on the spot, and sometimes that someone is going to make a mistake.

At least 99 percent of golf is played informally, and most of that 99 percent is played at match play. If there is a doubt or dispute about the Rules out on the course, the players should agree on the facts and then continue the match, even though they will not then be sure of the status of the match. They should get a decision as soon as they can without delaying play. Whoever is in charge of a golf course should authorize someone to make decisions, and it makes eminently good sense for that authority to be given to the golf professional.

A NOTE ON LOCAL RULES

Appendix I
LOCAL RULES

Rule 33-8 provides:

"The Committee may make and publish Local Rules for abnormal conditions if they are consistent with the policy of the Governing Authority for the country concerned as set forth in Appendix I to these Rules.

"A penalty imposed by a Rule of Golf shall not be waived by a Local Rule."

Among the matter for which Local Rules may be advisable are the following:

1. Obstructions

Clarifying the status of objects which may be obstructions (Rule 24).

Declaring any construction to be an integral part of the course and, accordingly, not an obstruction, *e.g.,* built-up sides of teeing grounds, putting greens and bunkers (Rules 24 and 33-2a).

2. Roads and Paths

Providing relief of the type afforded under Rule 24-2b from roads and paths not having artificial surfaces and sides if they could unfairly affect play.

3. Preservation of Course

Preservation of the course by defining areas, including turf nurseries an other parts of the course under cultivation, as ground under repair from which play is prohibited.

4. Unusual Damage to the Course

(other than as covered in Rule 25)

5. Water Hazards

Lateral Water Hazards. Clarifying the status of sections of water hazards which may be lateral water hazards (Rule 26).

Provisional Ball. Permitting play of a provisional ball for a ball which may be in a water hazard of such character that it would be impracticable to determine whether the ball is in the hazard or to do so would unduly delay play. In such case, if a provisional ball is played and the original ball is in a water hazard, the player may play the original ball as it lies or continue the provisional ball in play, but he may not proceed under Rule 26-1.

6. Defining Bounds and Margins

Specifying means used to define out of bounds, hazards,

water hazards, lateral water hazards and ground under repair.

7. Ball Drops

Establishment of special areas on which balls may be dropped when it is not feasible or practicable to proceed exactly in conformity with Rule 24-2b (immovable obstructions), Rule 25-1b or -1c (ground under repair), Rule 26-1 (water hazards and lateral water hazards) and Rule 28 (ball unplayable).

8. Temporary Conditions—Mud, Extreme Wetness

Temporary conditions which might interfere with proper playing of the game, including mud and extreme wetness warranting lifting an embedded ball anywhere through the green or removal of mud from a ball through the green.

Appendix I also suggests the text for a Local Rule authorizing lifting embedded balls "through the green" when a Committee feels that it would be unfair to confine the lifting of embedded balls to the putting green (see Rule 16-1c) and other closely mown areas (see Rule 25-2). Unless a more generous Local Rule is in effect, balls that are embedded in the rough may not be lifted without penalty.

"Preferred Lies" and "Winter Rules," which allow for moving the ball contrary to the principle expressed in Rule 13: "the ball shall be played as it lies," are also a subject in Appendix I. The USGA says it does not endorse such rules and will not interpret them, and points out quite correctly that they do fundamental damage to the principle that the ball should be played as it lies.

At the same time, it is recognized that conditions are sometimes so harsh that it's not possible to have a decent game without some form of "Preferred Lies" or "Winter Rules."

It is essential that this condition be covered by a detailed Local Rule. A notice posted only with the wording "Winter Rules" doesn't do the job. It suggests that the lie of the ball may be improved, but it doesn't answer the fundamental questions:

• May the lie of the ball be improved only in the fairway of the hole being played, on any fairway, through the green, in hazards—or sections of some hazards?

• When the ball is moved, may it be lifted, and if so, cleaned, or must it be moved only with a clubhead?

• How far may the ball be moved—six inches, one club-length, two club-lengths?

• When is the ball in play? Is it, for instance, in play as soon as it has been placed, or not in play until the player makes his next stroke?

The text of a Local Rule included in Appendix I reads: "A ball lying on a 'fairway' may be lifted and cleaned, without penalty, and placed within six inches of where it originally lay, not nearer the hole, and so as to preserve as nearly as possible the stance required to play from the original lie. After the ball has been so placed, it is in play, and if it moves after the player has addressed it, *the penalty shall be one stroke*—see Rule 18-2b."

RULES
QUIZ

RULES QUIZ

So now you know it all! You've plowed through my admonitions on Etiquette, the Definitions, the thirty-four Rules and Local Rules.

I hope you have enjoyed your labors and have profited from them. For your final exam I have included a quiz primarily devised by Tom Meeks, USGA Director of Rules and Competitions, to test the knowledge of students at a Rules of Golf workshop. It's meant to test your ability to *use* this book rather than your ability to snap off the correct answers. It's very much an open-book test, and each and every answer is readily available within the Rules proper.

The best way to join in the challenge of this quiz is to try to answer as many questions as possible within thirty minutes.

It is not intended to be an easy quiz. Anything but! If you can answer 40 of the 50 questions correctly within the thirty minutes, you're not far from being an expert. Anything better than that and you are one already! Good luck, and thanks for being an interested student.

The answers to the quiz appear on page 171.

1. Having overslept, a competitor in four-ball stroke play joins his partner and fellow-competitors between play of the 2nd and 3rd holes. What is the ruling?

_____(a) The competitor's side is penalized two strokes.

_____(b) The competitor's procedure was proper. He incurs no penalty.

_____(c) The competitor may join partner only if Committee waives the penalty for lateness.

_____(d) The competitor and his partner are disqualified.

_____(e) The competitor is penalized two strokes.

2. In four-ball stroke play, A and B are partners. By mistake, A starts his round with fifteen clubs. On the 14th green, A discovers his error. He immediately declares the excess club out of play. What is the ruling?

156

_____(a) A is penalized 4 strokes.

_____(b) Both A and B are penalized 4 strokes.

_____(c) Both A and B are penalized 2 strokes.

_____(d) A is penalized 2 strokes.

_____(e) A and B are disqualified.

3. Which of the following statements is true?

_____(a) Fences should not be used to define out of bounds.

_____(b) If a line on the ground is used to define out of bounds, it must be supplemented with white stakes.

_____(c) A ball is out of bounds when any part of it lies out of bounds.

_____(d) A ball is out of bounds when more than one-half of it lies out of bounds.

_____(e) An out of bounds line extends vertically upwards and downwards.

4. Which of the following statements is true?

_____(a) Between the play of two holes, a player may, for practice purposes, drive a ball from the side of the next tee to an out of bounds area.

_____(b) In stroke play, a competitor may test the surface of the 18th green before starting a round.

_____(c) A player may practice putting in the fairway while waiting for the group ahead to hole out.

_____(d) During play of a hole, a player may not tidy up the fairway by casually flicking a practice ball back onto an adjacent practice range.

_____(e) Between the play of two holes, a player may practice chip shots near the next tee.

5. In match play, a player has hit his ball into a bunker. His caddie arrived at the bunker first and went into it to retrieve a rake. While coming out of the bunker, the caddie raked his footprints. What penalty did the player incur?

_____(a) No penalty.

_____(b) Two-stroke penalty applied to the next hole.

_____(c) Loss-of-hole penalty applied to state of the match.

_____(d) One-stroke penalty.

_____(e) Loss of next hole.

6. The player's ball lies in a water hazard behind a crawfish mound. The player may:

_____(a) Treat the mound as a loose impediment.

_____(b) Drop the ball, without penalty, at the nearest point of maximum relief.

_____(c) Drop the ball, without penalty, within two club-lengths of the mound.

_____(d) Drop the ball, without penalty, within one club-length of the nearest point of relief.

_____(e) Play the ball as it lies or invoke the water hazard Rule since the Rules provide no free relief from the mound.

7. In which of the following areas do the margins extend vertically upwards?

_____(a) Bunkers and water hazards.

_____(b) Out of bounds and ground under repair.

_____(c) Bunkers and out of bounds.

_____(d) Ground under repair and water hazards.

_____(e) Out of bounds and water hazards.

8. The referee of a match attends a flagstick for A with A's knowledge, but A's ball does not strike the flagstick or the referee. What is the ruling?

_____(a) A loses the hole.

_____(b) A incurs a one-stroke penalty.

_____(c) A incurs no penalty.

_____(d) A must replay his shot with someone other than the referee attending the flagstick.

_____(e) A is disqualified.

9. In match play, a player accidentally moves his ball while searching for it in ground under repair. What is the ruling?

_____(a) The player incurs a penalty of one stroke, and the ball is played as it lies.

_____(b) The player incurs a penalty of one stroke, and the ball must be replaced.

_____(c) The player loses the hole.

_____(d) There is no penalty; the player must replace the ball and then decide whether or not to invoke the ground under repair Rule.

_____(e) There is no penalty; the player must replace the ball, unless he elects to invoke the ground under repair Rule.

10. In stroke play, A and B share a golf cart. A plays a shot and his ball hits the motionless cart in which B is sitting. What is the ruling?

_____(a) A incurs a two-stroke penalty and must play the ball as it lies.

_____(b) A incurs a two-stroke penalty and must replay the stroke.

_____(c) B incurs a two-stroke penalty and A must play the ball as it lies.

_____(d) No penalty is incurred since the cart was not in motion.

_____(e) A incurs a two-stroke penalty and has the option of playing his ball as it lies or replaying the stroke.

11. A competitor in stroke play missed a short putt and holed the ball by scraping it into the hole with his putter. What is the ruling?

_____(a) The stroke must be replayed, without penalty.

_____(b) The competitor incurs a two-stroke penalty and the stroke must be replayed.

_____(c) The competitor incurs a two-stroke penalty and the ball is holed.

_____(d) The competitor incurs a one-stroke penalty and the ball is holed.

_____(e) The competitor is disqualified.

12. A drove from the 1st tee and B played his second shot to the last green. The balls collided and A's ball came to rest out of bounds. B's ball came to rest in bounds. What is the ruling?

_____(a) A and B incur one-stroke penalties and must replay their shots.

_____(b) A and B incur two-stroke penalties and must replay their shots.

_____(c) There is no penalty for the balls colliding. Player B must play his ball as it lies. A incurs a stroke-and-distance penalty since his ball is out of bounds.

_____(d) There is no penalty. B must play his ball as it lies and A must replay his shot.

_____(e) A and B must replay their shots, without penalty.

13. A player drove his ball out of bounds. He teed another ball. In the act of addressing the ball, it fell off the tee but did not roll outside the teeing ground. What is the ruling?

_____(a) The player incurs a one-stroke penalty and must play the ball as it lies.

_____(b) The player incurs a two-stroke penalty and must play the ball as it lies.

_____(c) The player incurs no penalty and may re-tee the ball.

_____(d) The player incurs no penalty and must re-tee the ball.

_____(e) The player incurs a one-stroke penalty and must re-tee the ball.

14. In stroke play, a competitor returns his score card to the Committee. The hole-by-hole scores are correct; however, the total for one nine as recorded on the card by the competitor is one stroke higher than the actual total score. What is the ruling?

_____(a) There is no penalty; however, the incorrect total score stands.

_____(b) There is no penalty; the Committee must correct the error in addition.

_____(c) The competitor incurs a two-stroke penalty and he must correct the error.

_____(d) The competitor incurs a two-stroke penalty and the Committee must correct the error.

_____(e) The competitor is disqualified.

15. Which one of the following statements is correct?

_____(a) Regardless of the circumstances, before a player lifts his ball, the position of the ball must be marked.

_____(b) A small coin must be used to mark the position of a ball.

_____(c) A player must mark the position of his ball before lifting it on the putting green, but not before lifting it elsewhere.

_____(d) The position of a ball must be marked only before it is lifted under a Rule which requires it to be replaced.

_____(e) A player preparing to lift his ball need not mark the ball's position if he will be able, because of a blemish beside the ball, to replace the ball on the spot from which it was lifted.

16. In match play, a player's ball is behind a tree. He tries to play around the tree but the ball hits the tree, rebounds, hits the player and comes to rest in a very bad lie. What is the ruling?

———(a) In equity, there is no penalty because the player did not benefit as a result of the ball having struck him.

———(b) There is no penalty because the player did not purposely allow the ball to strike him.

———(c) The player is penalized one stroke and must play the ball as it lies.

———(d) The player loses the hole.

———(e) The player incurs a one-stroke penalty and must replay the stroke.

17. In a match between A and B, A by mistake plays a wrong ball at the 4th hole. He wins the hole with the wrong ball. The error is discovered by A and B during play of the next hole, and B claims the 4th hole. What is the ruling?

———(a) B should be disqualified for making an invalid claim.

———(b) B should be reprimanded by the Committee for making an invalid claim.

———(c) B's claim is valid.

———(d) B's claim is invalid because it was made after play had begun on the 5th hole.

———(e) The 4th hole should be decided by lot.

18. A player's ball lies just in bounds. In taking his normal stance, the player's feet would be out of bounds. There is an accumulation of rainwater out of bounds at the spot where his feet would be situated. The player claims relief under the casual water Rule. What is the ruling?

———(a) The player is entitled to relief under the casual water Rule.

———(b) The player is entitled to relief but, in equity, he must drop the ball at a spot which would result in his having to stand out of bounds to play his next stroke.

———(c) The player must declare the ball unplayable.

———(d) The player must declare the ball out of bounds.

———(e) The player is not entitled to relief, without penalty, from the water.

19. A's ball lies just outside a water hazard. B's ball is in the hazard. A bridge in the hazard interferes with both A's swing and B's. Which one of the following statements is correct?

———(a) Neither A nor B is entitled to free relief from the bridge.

———(b) Both A and B are entitled to free relief from the bridge.

_____(c) A is entitled to free relief from the bridge, but not B.

_____(d) B is entitled to free relief from the bridge, but not A.

_____(e) A is entitled to free relief from the bridge, but he must drop his ball in the hazard.

20. In stroke play, A finished his round, went back onto the course and began caddying for and giving advice to B, a friend. B had not had a caddie up to that point. What is the ruling?

_____(a) B incurred a penalty of two strokes each time A gave him advice.

_____(b) A should be disqualified.

_____(c) Neither A nor B is subject to penalty.

_____(d) Both A and B should be disqualified.

_____(e) B should be disqualified.

21. Which of the following is the Committee not required to define accurately?

_____(a) Ground under repair.

_____(b) The margins of a lateral water hazard.

_____(c) Out of bounds.

_____(d) Casual water.

_____(e) The margins of water hazards.

22. Which one of the following is an immovable obstruction?

_____(a) A fence defining out of bounds.

_____(b) An artificially surfaced path situated out of bounds.

_____(c) A stile attached to a boundary fence.

_____(d) A rake left in a bunker.

_____(e) Part of a boundary fence within the boundary line.

23. While playing the 1st hole, which area of the course is not covered by the term "through the green?"

_____(a) The putting green of the 1st hole.

_____(b) The teeing ground of the 2nd hole.

_____(c) The rough between the 2nd and 3rd fairways.

_____(d) The fairway of the 2nd hole.

_____(e) Ground under repair on the 1st fairway.

24. In stroke play, which of the following is not an outside agency?

_____(a) The caddie of a fellow-competitor.

_____(b) The golf cart of a fellow-competitor.

_____(c) The competitor's caddie.

_____(d) An observer.

_____(e) A marker.

25. Which of the following is not a loose impediment?

_____(a) A leaf adhering to a ball.

_____(b) Snow.

_____(c) A worm.

_____(d) Sand on the putting green.

_____(e) An insect.

26. What is automatically ground under repair under the Rules of Golf?

_____(a) Cracks in the earth.

_____(b) A divot hole.

_____(c) A dry drainage ditch.

_____(d) A hole made in removing a tree stump.

_____(e) A rut made by a tractor.

27. During a stroke play round, play was suspended by the Committee due to weather. One group of competitors, having hit their tee shots, was in the middle of the 18th fairway. Which of the following is incorrect?

_____(a) The competitors may immediately discontinue play.

_____(b) The competitors may play their second shots and then discontinue play.

_____(c) The competitors may complete the hole.

_____(d) The competitors may discontinue play after hitting their second shots and, if the weather improves, complete the hole before the Committee orders a resumption of play.

_____(e) The competitors may discontinue play, mark and lift their balls, and when play is resumed substitute new balls for the balls they lifted.

163

28. In stroke play, a player's ball lies in grass overhanging a bunker. The player removes a leaf, which is situated near his ball, from the bunker and grounds his club lightly in the bunker before playing the stroke. What is the ruling?

_____(a) No penalty.

_____(b) One-stroke penalty.

_____(c) Two-stroke penalty.

_____(d) Four-stroke penalty.

_____(e) Disqualification for a serious breach.

29. A and B are playing together in stroke play. A hits B's ball by mistake, which was lying in the fairway. What is the ruling?

_____(a) B must drop a ball at the spot where his original ball lay. A must play the correct ball, and must count all strokes taken with both balls.

_____(b) B must drop a ball at the spot where his original ball lay. A incurs a two-stroke penalty and must play the correct ball, counting all strokes taken with both balls.

_____(c) B must place a ball at the spot where his original ball lay. A incurs a two-stroke penalty and must play the correct ball, counting all strokes taken with both balls.

_____(d) B must place a ball at the spot where his original ball lay. A incurs a two-stroke penalty, must play the correct ball and count only strokes taken with the correct ball.

_____(e) B must drop a ball at the spot from which his original ball was played. A incurs a two-stroke penalty, must play the correct ball and count only strokes taken with the correct ball.

30. In how many situtations is the stroke-and-distance penalty the player's sole option?

_____(a) 1.

_____(b) 2.

_____(c) 3.

_____(d) 4.

_____(e) 5.

31. A player addresses the ball and starts his backswing. During the backswing, the ball moves. The player continues the swing and hits the ball. What is the ruling?

_____(a) Two-stroke penalty; ball is played as it lies.

_____(b) Two-stroke penalty; ball is replaced.

_____(c) One-stroke penalty; ball is played as it lies.

_____(d) One-stroke penalty; ball is replaced.

_____(e) No penalty; ball is played as it lies.

32. What is the ruling if a player's ball breaks into pieces as a result of a stroke?

_____(a) There is no penalty; the stroke must be replayed.

_____(b) The stroke counts; the player may substitute another ball at the spot where the largest piece came to rest.

_____(c) The stroke counts; another ball must be placed at the spot from which the previous stroke was played.

_____(d) The stroke counts; another ball must be dropped as near as possible to the spot from which the previous stroke was played.

_____(e) The stroke counts; another ball may be substituted at the spot where any piece of the original ball came to rest.

33. In stroke play, a player drops a ball. En route to the ground, the ball strikes his foot. What is the procedure?

_____(a) The ball must be re-dropped, without penalty; if it touches his foot on the re-drop, it must be placed where it first struck the ground when re-dropped.

_____(b) The ball must be re-dropped, without penalty; if it touches his foot on the re-drop it must be re-dropped again, without penalty.

_____(c) The ball is in play, and the player incurs a one-stroke penalty.

_____(d) The ball is in play, and the player incurs a two-stroke penalty.

_____(e) The ball must be re-dropped, and the player incurs a two-stroke penalty.

34. In stroke play, a competitor is playing from just off the green. His fellow-competitor's caddie is attending the flagstick at the competitor's request. The competitor plays and the fellow-competitor's caddie is unable to remove the flagstick because it sticks in the pocket. The ball strikes the flagstick. What is the ruling?

_____(a) The stroke must be replayed, without penalty.

_____(b) The ball shall be played as it lies; there is no penalty as the ball was played from off the green.

_____(c) The ball shall be played as it lies, and the competitor incurs a two-stroke penalty.

_____(d) The fellow-competitor incurs a two-stroke penalty; the competitor replays, without penalty.

_____(e) The fellow-competitor incurs a two stroke penalty; the competitor's ball shall be played as it lies.

35. In which circumstance is a player prohibited from cleaning a lifted ball?

_____(a) When the ball is lifted for relief from an unplayable lie.

_____(b) When the ball is lifted for relief from an immovable obstruction.

_____(c) When the ball is lifted for relief from casual water.

_____(d) When the ball is lifted for relief from a wrong green.

_____(e) When the ball is lifted through the green because it interferes with another player's play.

36. Which one of the following statements is false?

_____(a) A player, playing in the rain, may apply resin to the grip of his club to keep his hands from slipping.

_____(b) Sand is a loose impediment on the putting green, but not elsewhere on the course.

_____(c) A ball lying on a line defining ground under repair with no part of it overhanging the inside edge of the line is in the ground under repair.

_____(d) There are only two regulations governing golf balls. One restricts the size of the ball and the other the weight.

_____(e) When a stroke play event is to be played on consecutive days, it is not permissible to practice on the competition course between rounds.

37. Which one of the following statements is false?

_____(a) There is no penalty for practicing on the competition course on any day of a match play competition.

_____(b) If a player plays a practice stroke from a bunker after completing the 1st hole in match play, he loses the 1st hole.

_____(c) If a player plays a practice stroke during play of the 2nd hole in match play, he loses the 2nd hole.

_____(d) There is no penalty for playing a practice stroke on the putting green of the hole just completed.

_____(e) In stroke play, a player incurs a two-stroke penalty for practicing on the 5th green while waiting to tee off on the 2nd hole.

38. Which one of the following statements is false?

_____(a) A player may not borrow a club from a fellow-competitor in his group if one of his clubs is broken in the normal course of play.

_____(b) The forward movement of the club made with the intention of fairly striking at and moving the ball is defined as a "stroke."

_____(c) In teeing, the ball may be placed on sand in order to raise it off the ground.

_____(d) The number of holes in a stipulated round is eighteen unless a smaller number is authorized by the Committee.

_____(e) Partners may share clubs, provided the total number of clubs carried by the partners so sharing does not exceed fourteen.

39. Which one of the following statements is true?

_____(a) A player who lifts his ball under a Rule may, in any circumstances, clean the ball before putting it back into play.

_____(b) A player is dormie when he is four down with four holes to play.

_____(c) When a ball overhangs the edge of the hole, the player incurs no penalty if he waits thirty seconds for it to fall into the hole, and it falls in.

_____(d) A paper cup may not be removed from a bunker.

_____(e) There is no such thing as casual water in a water hazard.

40. In stroke play, a player brushes aside leaves on his line of putt with his cap or a towel. What is the ruling?

_____(a) No penalty.

_____(b) One-stroke penalty.

_____(c) Two-stroke penalty.

_____(d) Disqualification.

_____(e) No penalty, but the leaves must be replaced.

41. In match play, a player's ball is deflected by his opponents' golf bag. What is the ruling?

_____(a) No penalty; the ball must be played as it lies.

_____(b) No penalty; the ball must be replayed.

_____(c) The player loses the hole.

167

_____(d) The opponent loses the hole.

_____(e) There is no penalty; the player may either play the ball as it lies or replay the stroke.

42. In match play, A by mistake starts with fifteen clubs in his bag. He wins the first three holes and, walking to the 4th tee, he discovers his error. What is the ruling?

_____(a) A is disqualified.

_____(b) He loses each hole on which he carried fifteen clubs; thus, he is 3 down instead of 3 up.

_____(c) A loses the first two holes instead of winning them. Thus, he is 1 down.

_____(d) A incurs a penalty of two holes. The penalty is applied to the state of the match at the time the breach was discovered. Thus, A is 1 up.

_____(e) A incurs no penalty as he did not deliberately start with fifteen clubs.

43. A ball lies in a paper cup in a hazard. What is the procedure?

_____(a) The cup may not be removed. A cup may be removed only if it is not in a hazard.

_____(b) The cup may be removed. The ball must be dropped within two club-lengths of the spot from which it was moved, but not nearer the hole, without penalty.

_____(c) The cup may be removed. The ball must be placed on the exact spot from which it was moved.

_____(d) The cup may be removed. The ball must be dropped in the hazard as near as possible to the spot from which it was moved, but not nearer the hole, without penalty.

_____(e) The cup may be removed. The ball must be placed in the hazard as near as possible to the spot from which it was moved, but not nearer the hole, without penalty.

44. The player incurs a one-stroke penalty and the ball must be replaced in which one of the following situations?

_____(a) A player, requested to lift his ball due to interference, accidentally kicks the ball when approaching it.

_____(b) A player causes his ball to move while measuring to determine which ball is farther from the hole.

_____(c) The opponent accidentally kicks the player's ball. The player then plays his ball as it lies.

_____(d) A fellow-competitor accidentally causes the player's ball to move during search.

_____(e) A player, who thinks his ball is on the green when it's actually on the collar, marks and lifts his ball.

45. In stroke play, A's ball lies in a lateral water hazard. He determines the point where the ball last crossed the hazard margin and drops his ball three club-lengths from that point. Before A plays, B, a fellow-competitor, tells A that he (A) should have dropped within two club-lengths. What is the ruling?

_____(a) No penalty provided A then re-drops within two club-lengths.

_____(b) One-stroke penalty; A must play the ball as it lies.

_____(c) One-stroke penalty; A must then drop within two club-lengths.

_____(d) Two-stroke penalty; A must play the ball as it lies.

_____(e) Two-stroke penalty; A must then drop within two club-lengths.

46. Which one of the following statements is correct with respect to when a player may play a provisional ball?

_____(a) If the original ball might be lost through the green or lost in a water hazard.

_____(b) If the original ball might be lost through the green or unplayable.

_____(c) If the original ball might be out of bounds or unplayable.

_____(d) If the original ball might be out of bounds or lost through the green.

_____(e) If the original ball might be out of bounds, lost through the green, unplayable or lost in a water hazard.

47. In stroke play, a competitor tees his ball slightly in front of the tee-markers and plays. After he plays his third shot, a fellow-competitor calls the competitor's attention to the error. What is the ruling?

_____(a) The competitor is penalized two strokes and continues play with the ball played from in front of the tee-markers.

_____(b) The competitor is penalized two strokes and must return to the tee and play from within the teeing ground.

_____(c) There is no penalty since the competitor did not tee off more than two club-lengths in front of the tee-markers. He must continue to play with the ball played from in front of the tee-markers.

_____(d) The competitor must count the three strokes played, return to the tee and play from within the teeing ground.

_____(e) The competitor is disqualified since he did not rectify his error before playing his second stroke.

48. In match play, a player and his opponent exchange balls during the play of a hole, and it cannot be determined who played the wrong ball first. What is the ruling?

_____(a) The hole should be played out with the balls exchanged.

_____(b) The players should return to the tee and replay the hole.

_____(c) Both players should be disqualified.

_____(d) The winner of the hole should be decided by lot.

_____(e) The hole should be considered halved.

49. In a four-ball match, a player played his second shot to the green although it was an opponent's turn to play. What is the ruling?

_____(a) There is no penalty; the opponents have the right to require the player to replay in proper order.

_____(b) There is no penalty; the stroke shall not be replayed.

_____(c) There is a one-stroke penalty; the stroke shall not be replayed.

_____(d) There is a one-stroke penalty; the opponents have the right to require the player to replay in proper order.

_____(e) The player who played out of turn is disqualified for the hole.

50. In a four-ball match, a player putts and his ball strikes his partner's ball and moves it. What is the ruling?

_____(a) The player and his partner lose the hole.

_____(b) The player is disqualified for the hole; the partner is not penalized.

_____(c) There is no penalty; the partner must replace his ball.

_____(d) There is no penalty; the balls must be played as they lie.

_____(e) There is no penalty; the partner has the option of playing his ball as it lies or replacing it.

ANSWERS

1. b (Rule 31-2)
2. b (Rule 31-3)
3. e (Definition—Out of Bounds)
4. e (Rule 7-2)
5. a (Rule 13-4, Exception 3)
6. e (Rule 25-1c(ii), Exception)
7. e (Definitions—Out of Bounds and Water Hazard)
8. c (Definition—Referee, Rule 17-1)
9. e (Rule 12-1)
10. a (Rule 19-2b)
11. c (Rule 14-1)
12. c (Rule 19-5)
13. c (Rule 11-3)
14. b (Rule 33-5)
15. d (Rule 20-1)
16. d (Rule 19-2a)
17. c (Rule 34-1a, Rule 2-5 and Rule 9-2)
18. e (Definition—Casual Water and Rule 25-1)
19. c (Rule 24-2 note)
20. c (Rule 6-4)
21. d (Rule 33-2a)
22. c (Definition—Obstructions)
23. a (Definition—Through the Green)
24. c (Definition—Outside Agency)
25. a (Definition—Loose Impediment)
26. d (Definition—Ground Under Repair)
27. d (Rule 6-8b and -8c)
28. a (Definition—Bunker)
29. d (Rule 15-3)
30. b (Out of Bounds and Lost Ball)
31. c (Rule 14-5 and Rule 18-2b)
32. a (Rule 5-3)
33. b (Rule 20-2a)
34. c (Rule 17-3a)
35. e (Rule 21(c))
36. d (Rule 5-1)
37. b (Rule 7-2, Penalty)
38. a (Rule 4-4a and -4b)
39. e (Definition—Casual Water)
40. c (Rule 16-1a(i))
41. e (Rule 19-3)
42. d (Rule 4-4, Penalty)
43. d (Rule 24-1b)
44. e (Rule 18-2a)
45. a (Rule 20-6)
46. d (Rule 27-2)
47. b (Rule 11-4b)
48. a (Rule 15-2)
49. a (Rule 10-1c)
50. c (Rule 18-5 and Rule 19-5)

INDEX TO THE RULES OF GOLF

C

D

E

F

G

M

O

T

U

W

For more information on the Rules of Gulf, the following publications are available for purchase from the United States Golf Association:

The Rules of Golf:
as approved by the United States Golf Association. Booklet; $1.00. (special rates for quantity orders: 250–999, 80¢; 1,000–9,999, 70¢; 10,000 and up, 55¢)

Decisions on the Rules of Golf by the United States Golf Association and the Royal and Ancient Golf Club of St. Andrews, Scotland:
interpretations of the Rules of Golf, including complete Rules and index; over 500 pages, softcover; $15.00

Golf Rules in Brief:
a six-page pamphlet featuring some basic Rules in easy-to-understand language; 50¢, $25.00 per 100.

Help in the Interpretation of the Rules of Golf:
a publication of the Royal and Ancient Golf Club of St. Andrews. $10.00.

What to Do About Obstructions:
information on proper procedures under the Rules pertaining to obstructions. $1.00, $50.00 per 100.

At Sea in a Water Hazard:
a pamphlet of Rules pertaining to water hazards. $1.00, $50.00 per 100.

Please include shipping and handling charges as follows:

Total Amount of Order	Shipping and Handling Charges
up to $4.99	$0.50
$5 to $9.99	$1.00
$10 to $24.99	$1.50
$25 to $40.00	$3.00
$50 to $249.99	$5.00
$250 to $499.99	$10.00
$500 and above	Actual shipping will be charged

To order, send check made out to the USGA to:

USGA Order Department
P.O. Box 3000
Far Hills, NJ 07931-3000

New Jersey residents, please add 6% sales tax.
Prices subject to change.

Writing and interpreting the Rules of Golf are just two of the services of the United States Golf Association. The USGA also conducts 13 national championships, provides national handicapping and course rating systems, tests balls and clubs for conformity, maintains golf's most complete museum and library collection, and conducts turfgrass research and course maintenance programs. The USGA performs these and other services for the good of the game.

For information on how you can support the USGA, call:
1-800-223-0041

SUPPORT THE USGA ASSOCIATES PROGRAM

About the Authors

Among **Tom Watson**'s many victories are the U.S. Open in 1982, the Masters in 1977 and 1981, and the British Open in 1975, 1977, 1980, 1982 and 1983. He was the PGA Player of the Year for four consecutive years (five times overall). A graduate of Stanford University, he lives in Mission Hills, Kansas, when he is not touring.

Frank Hannigan, Senior Executive Director of the United States Golf Association, has helped conduct more than a hundred national championships and international competitions. He has a second career as a prizewinning golf writer and frequently appears as a special commentator on the Rules of Golf during network golf telecasts.